"So many Christian parents fall int[   ]hearts of their children what only grace can accomplish. Armed with threats, manipulation, and guilt, they attempt to create change that only the cross of Jesus Christ makes possible. It is so encouraging to read a parenting book that points parents to the grace of the cross and shows them how to be instruments of that grace in the lives of their children."

Paul David Tripp, President, Paul Tripp Ministries

"In our human attempts to raise good and godly kids, we often forget that God extended his best grace to us. We are not full of grace on our own; we desperately need his grace. Elyse Fitzpatrick and her daughter, Jessica, provide a great tool to guide parents down the road of gracious parenting. I commend it to you."

James MacDonald, Senior Pastor, Harvest Bible Chapel; radio teacher, *Walk in the Word*

"Elyse Fitzpatrick continues her never-ending quest to churn out grace-filled, Christ-centered, gospel-saturated books. And now she's done it again with her daughter, Jessica, coauthoring this excellent parenting book. If you are a parent, get online and order your copy of *Give Them Grace* today!"

Deepak Reju, Pastor of Biblical Counseling and Families, Capitol Hill Baptist Church, Washington, DC

"The authors—mother and daughter—remind us that parenting is not only hard but also impossible. Yes, we need to nurture, teach, discipline, train, pray, and model, but we must not depend on our parenting skills to change the hearts of our children. Instead, they counsel parents to 'rely on the faithfulness of Jesus, our great high priest, to change their hearts.' Grace for both parents and children flows through the pages of this book. I only wish I had read it at the beginning of my parenting instead of at the end."

Rose Marie Miller, missionary; speaker; author, *From Fear to Freedom*

"This is not just a book on parenting; this is deep training in the gospel. Elyse Fitzpatrick shows parents how to model themselves after the heavenly Father, who changed his children not by wrath and the law but by grace. A lot of books talk about gospel-centeredness in theory; this book shows you how to apply it to one of life's most important relationships."

J. D. Greear, Pastor, Summit Church; author, *GOSPEL: Recovering the Power that Made Christianity Revolutionary*

GIVE THEM
grace

GIVE THEM
grace

Dazzling Your Kids with the Love of Jesus

Elyse M. Fitzpatrick
& Jessica Thompson

CROSSWAY®

WHEATON, ILLINOIS

Give Them Grace: Dazzling Your Kids with the Love of Jesus

Copyright © 2011 by Elyse M. Fitzpatrick and Jessica Thompson

Published by Crossway
>   1300 Crescent Street
>   Wheaton, Illinois 60187

Cover design: Amy Bristow

Cover image: © Oliver Rossi/Corbis

Typesetting: Lakeside Design Plus

First printing 2011

Printed in the United States of America

Trade paperback ISBN 978-1-4335-2009-9
PDF ISBN 978-1-4335-2010-5
Mobipocket ISBN 978-1-4335-2022-8
ePub ISBN 978-1-4335-2023-5

Library of Congress Cataloging-in-Publication Data

Fitzpatrick, Elyse, 1950–
    Give them grace : dazzling your kids with the love of Jesus / Elyse M. Fitzpatrick and Jessica Thompson.
        p. cm.
    Includes bibliographical references and index.
    ISBN 978-1-4335-2009-9 (tp)
    1. Child rearing—Religious aspects—Christianity.
2. Law and gospel. I. Thompson, Jessica, 1975– II. Title.
BV4529.F559   2011
248.8'45—dc22   2010045945

Crossway is a publishing ministry of Good News Publishers.

VP		24	23	22	21	20	19	18	17	
24	23	22	21	20	19	18	17	16	15	

To
my dear mother, Rosemary.
—Elyse

To
my husband, Cody,
with thanks for supporting me in this endeavor
and for loving Christ, our children, the church, and me.
I love you.
And to my parents,
whose love for each other and for Christ has changed me.
—Jessica

To
Kei, dear friend
whose words were so helpful
and whose life spoke volumes.

—Elyse and Jessica

God is able to make all grace abound
to you . . . so that you may abound in every good work.
2 Corinthians 9:8

Contents

Are You a Christian Parent?

Jessica heard the terrifying scream emanating from the playroom. Frantically rushing out of the bathroom (every mom knows what this is like!), she found her eldest son, Wesley (then four), seated atop his little brother pounding away. As she forcefully yanked Wesley off his brother, she pled with him, "Wesley, you must love your brother!"

"But he makes me so mad! I can't love him!" Wesley replied through angry tears.

We're sure you, as a parent, can easily imagine a situation like that one. Now, if you were Wesley's dad or mom, how would you have answered him? Or, to put a finer point on it, how do you think a *Christian* parent should respond to a child who is angry, disobedient, and hopeless? And should a Christian's response differ significantly from what we might hear from a loving Mormon mom or a conscientious Jewish father? Sure, all parents would undoubtedly have restrained their son and told him that beating up his little brother is inappropriate behavior. But then what? What would come next? Is there something that would make a Christian's response distinctly Christian?

When we were raising our daughter, Jessica (along with her brothers, James and Joel), I (Elyse) would have answered Wesley's "I can't love my brother!" in this way: "Oh, yes, you can and you will! God says that you must love your brother, and you better start—or else!" Would your answer have been different from mine? If so, in what way, and how would you know if your reply was a distinctly Christian one? After all, it's obvious that although we're Christian parents, it doesn't necessarily follow that our parenting is essentially Christian. Frequently it's something else entirely.

Where Did Those Easy Steps Get To?

Because parenting is one of those learn-as-you-go endeavors, books and seminars about doing it well are in high demand. And because most of us are stretched for time, we especially appreciate teachers and writers who give us a tidy list of three foolproof steps we can memorize in an afternoon while the kids enjoy a play-date with their friends. We know that learning how to answer questions like the one posed above is one of the primary reasons you've picked up this book. You're wondering what to say when it seems like your kids just aren't getting it and seem, in fact, to be going in the wrong direction. How should a Christian dad or mom respond to the disobedience, selfishness, hopelessness, or sullenness that so frequently marks the lives of our children? Conversely, how should we respond when they seem to be outwardly compliant but are obviously proud and hypocritical?

We understand. We know you need answers. You want to be a faithful parent or you wouldn't be bothering with this book. Like you, we long to be faithful parents, too. But both Jessica and I (Elyse) are not only mothers who, along with our husbands, want to be faithful parents; we are also people who have been transformed by the message of the gospel of grace. So, yes, this book will answer many of your "How am I supposed to respond to *that* kind of behavior?" questions. But that's not its primary purpose.

This book will provide you with something more than a three-step formula for successful parenting. That's because even though it might seem counter-intuitive, none of us need more law. In this case, law might masquerade as "easy steps," "hints for success," or even "secret formulas," but make no mistake: at heart it is law. Mormons, Muslims, and moralistic atheists all share the belief that law can perfect us, but Christians don't. Christians know that the law can't save us; what we need is a Savior. We need a Savior because every one of us has already demonstrated that we don't respond well to rules (Rom. 3:23). We've been given a perfect law (Rom. 7:12) but none of us—no, not one—has obeyed it (Rom. 3:10). Why would we think that our success rate would be any different if we just had different laws?

In light of our dismal record, it should be obvious that our salvation and the salvation of our children must come from someone else. This person has to give us something other than more rules to obey. But what else is there? There is grace. And what he brings us is simply that—grace. Grace is what we want to give to you, too, so that you can give it to your children in turn. Our salvation (and our kids' as well) is by grace alone through faith alone in Christ alone. Grace alone.

Most of us are painfully aware that we're not perfect parents. We're also deeply grieved that we don't have perfect kids. But the remedy to our mutual imperfections isn't more law, even if it seems to produce tidy or polite children. Christian children (and their parents) don't need to learn to be "nice." They need death and resurrection and a Savior who has gone before them as a faithful high priest, who was a child himself, and who lived and died perfectly in their place. They need a Savior who extends the offer of complete forgiveness, total righteousness, and indissoluble adoption to all who will believe. This is the message we all need. We need the gospel of grace and the grace of the gospel. Children can't use the law any more than we can, because they will respond to it the same way we do. They'll ignore it or bend it or obey it outwardly for selfish purposes, but this one thing is certain: they won't obey it from the heart, because they can't. That's why Jesus had to die.

We understand that right about now you might be getting a little uncomfortable with what we are saying. You might be wondering what we mean by the "law" and why we are saying that our kids don't need it. Don't be discouraged. We've anticipated your questions, and we'll answer them in the chapters to come. We are not going to leave you without a way to respond to and train your children, although it might be very different from the way you're doing that right now.

Have They Heard the Message?

Christians know that the gospel is the message unbelievers need to hear. We tell them that they can't earn their way into heaven and that they have to trust in Jesus alone for their goodness. But then something odd happens when we start training the miniature unbelievers in our own home. We forget everything we know about the deadliness of relying on our own goodness and we teach them that Christianity is all about their behavior and whether, on any given day, God is pleased or displeased with them. It's no wonder that so many of them (some estimates are as high as 88 percent but *none* are under 60 percent[1]) are lost to utter rebellion or to works-based cults such as Mormonism as soon as they are free to make an independent choice.

There is no easy way to say it, but it must be said: parents and churches are not passing on a robust Christian faith and an accompanying commitment to the church. We can take some solace in the fact that many grown children do eventually return. But Christian parents and churches need to ask the hard question, "What is it about our faith commitment that does not find root in the lives of our children?"[2]

It's the premise of this book that the primary reason the majority of kids from Christian homes stray from the faith is that they never really heard it or had it to begin with. They were taught that God wants them to be good, that poor Jesus is sad when they disobey, and that asking Jesus into their heart is the breadth and depth of the gospel message. Scratch the surface of the faith of the young people around you and you'll find a disturbing deficiency of understanding of even the most basic tenets of Christianity.

This is illustrated by a conversation I recently had with a young woman in her early twenties who had been raised in a Christian home and had attended church for most of her life. After assuring me that she was, indeed, saved, I asked her, "What does it mean to be a Christian?"

She replied, "It means that you ask Jesus into your heart."

"Yes, all right, but what does that mean?"

"It means that you ask Jesus to forgive you."

"Okay, but what do you ask him to forgive you for?"

"Bad things? I guess you ask him to forgive you for bad things, um, the sins you do."

"Like what?"

A deer in the headlights stared back at me. I thought I'd try a different tack.

"Why would Jesus forgive you?"

She fidgeted. "Um, because you ask him?"

Okay, I thought, *I'll try again.*

"What do you think God wants you to know?"

She beamed. "He wants me to know that I should love myself and that there's nothing I can't do if I think I can."

"And what does God want from you?" I asked.

"He wants me to do good stuff."

"Like?"

The deer reappeared. "You know, be nice to others and don't hang around with bad people."

Be Good for Goodness' Sake

Of course, you might say that this superficiality is an aberration and not typical of the kids in your home or church. We hope you're right. But we all have to admit that if a majority of our children are leaving the faith as soon as they can, something has gone terribly wrong. Certainly the faith that has empowered the persecuted church for two millennia isn't as thin and boring as "Say you're sorry," "Be nice," and "Don't be like *them*." Why would anyone want to deny himself, lay down his life, or suffer for something as inane as that? Aside from the "Ask Jesus into your heart" part, how does this message differ from what any unchurched child or Jewish young person would hear every day?

Let's face it: most of our children believe that God is happy if they're "good for goodness' sake." We've transformed the holy, terrifying, magnificent, and loving God of the Bible into Santa and his elves. And instead of transmitting the gloriously liberating and life-changing truths of the gospel, we have taught our children that what God wants from them is morality. We have told them that *being good* (at least outwardly) is the be-all and end-all of their faith. This isn't the gospel; we're not handing down Christianity. We need much less of *Veggie Tales* and Barney and tons more of the radical, bloody, scandalous message of God made man and crushed by his Father for our sin.

This other thing that we're giving them has a name—it's called "moralism." Here's how one seminary professor described his childhood experience in church:

> The preachers I regularly heard in the . . . church in which I was raised tended to interpret and preach Scripture without Christ as the central . . . focus. Characters like Abraham and Paul were commended as models of sincere faith and loyal obedience. . . . On the other hand, men like Adam and Judas were criticized as the antithesis of proper moral behavior. Thus Scripture became nothing more than a source book for moral lessons on Christian living whether good or bad. [3]

When we change the story of the Bible from the gospel of grace to a book of moralistic teachings like Aesop's fables, all sorts of things go wrong. Unbelieving children are encouraged to display the fruit of the Holy Spirit even though they are spiritually dead in their trespasses and sins (Eph. 2:1). Unrepentant children are taught to say that they're sorry and ask for forgiveness even though they've never tasted true godly sorrow. Unregenerate kids are told that they are pleasing to God because they have achieved some "moral victory." Good manners have been elevated to the level of Christian righteousness. Parents discipline their kids until they evidence a prescribed form of contrition, and others work hard at keeping their children from the wickedness in the world, assuming that the wickedness within their children has been handled because they prayed a prayer one time at Bible club.

If our "faith commitments" haven't taken root in our children, could it be because they have not consistently heard them? Instead of the gospel of grace, we've given them daily baths in a "sea of narcissistic moralism,"[4] and they respond to law the same way we do: they run for the closest exit as soon as they can.

Moralistic parenting occurs because most of us have a wrong view of the Bible. The story of the Bible isn't a story about making good little boys and girls better. As Sally Lloyd-Jones writes in *The Jesus Storybook Bible*:

> Now, some people think the Bible is a book of rules, telling you what you should and shouldn't do. The Bible certainly does have some rules in it. They show you how life works best. But the Bible isn't mainly about you and what you should be doing. It's about God and what he has done. Other people think the Bible is a book of heroes, showing you people you should copy. The Bible does have some heroes in it, but . . . most of the people in the Bible aren't heroes at all. They make some big mistakes (sometimes on purpose), they get afraid and run away. At times they are downright mean. *No, the Bible isn't a book of rules, or a book of heroes.* The Bible is most of all a Story. It's an adventure story about a young Hero who comes from a far country to win back his lost treasure. It's a love story about a brave Prince who leaves his palace, his throne—everything—to rescue the one he loves. It's like the most wonderful of fairy tales that has come true in real life.[5]

This is the story that our children need to hear and, like us, they need to hear it over and over again.

You're a Christian Parent but Is Your Parenting Christian?

Grace, or the free favor that has been lavished on us through Christ, ought to make our parenting radically different from what unbelievers do. That's because the good news of God's grace is meant to permeate and transform every relationship we have, including our relationship with our children. All the typical ways we construct to get things done and get others to do our bidding are simply obliterated by a gospel message that tells us that we are all (parents and children) both *radically sinful* and *radically loved*. At the deepest level of what we do as parents, we should hear the heartbeat of a loving, grace-giving Father who freely adopts rebels and transforms them into loving sons and daughters. If this is not the message that your children hear from you, if the message that you send them on a daily basis is about being good so that you won't be disappointed, then the gospel needs to transform your parenting, too.

And now back to the little vignette we opened our introduction with. You'll remember that we left Wesley after he had just cried out, "I can't love my brother!" The Christian response to his cry isn't what I (Elyse) would have said: "Oh, yes, you can and you will. The Bible says you have to, so you can." No, the Christian response to a statement like "I can't love my brother!" is something more along these lines:

Exactly! I am so glad to hear you say that, because it shows me that God is working in you. It is true that God commands you to love your brother, Wesley, but you can't. That is the bad news, but that is not all the news there is. The rest of the news is so exciting! You can't love your brother like God is asking you to, so you need a Rescuer to help you. And the really great news is that God has already sent one! His name is Jesus! Jesus has perfectly loved you and perfectly loved his brothers for you, fulfilling the law to love in your place. If you believe in him, he doesn't punish you, the way you were punishing and beating up your brother. Instead of punishing you, he took all the punishment you deserve when he died on the cross for you. He knows how angry you are. He knows that there are times you are hateful and selfish with your brother. But he has loved you in spite of your sin. And because of this, Wesley, because of the way you have been lavishly loved, if you believe in him, you will grow to love your brother more and more. Because of Jesus alone, because of what He has already done for you, you can learn how to love if you believe that he will be that loving with you. But you'll never be able to do this on your own.

After sharing soul-comforting words like those, Jessica continued with a time of discipline and prayer for Wesley that God would grant him faith to believe that the Rescuer he needed loved him, would forgive him, and would help him love others, too.

He Is the Faithful Father

Please don't misunderstand. We don't always respond with grace like this, nor will our children always listen when we do. Sometimes they roll their eyes; other times they pretend to listen but don't hear a word we say. Sometimes we are sure they are thinking, "Grace, gospel, blah, blah, blah." Frequently, what might have been a wonderful grace moment becomes nothing more than discipline and prayer for grace. Sometimes we are distracted or in a hurry or discouraged or apathetic, and we don't have the time or the inclination to give grace to our children. Sometimes we ignore them and wish we could have an afternoon alone. We are just like you.

Although we long to be faithful parents, we also rest in the truth that our faithfulness is not what will save our children. Giving grace to our children is not another formula that guarantees their salvation or obedience. Grace-parenting is not another law for you to master to perfect your parenting or your children. Our children will be saved *only* through the faithfulness of the Holy Spirit, who works at the direction of our faithful heavenly Father. He's the faithful, powerful, soul-transforming One. Yes, he may use us as means to accomplish his purpose, but salvation is *entirely* of the Lord (Jonah 2:9).

If the gospel message that we have presented in this introduction is something new or foreign to you, please do turn to Appendix 3 at the back of this book. Wouldn't it be wonderful to know the kind of love we've been talking about and to be able to rest in God's faithfulness to enable you to parent your children well?

Finally, when the word *I* appears, it's Elyse talking (unless otherwise indicated). Jessica and I have collaborated on this project for years, and her "feet on the ground" perspective is what has made this book something more than the musings of a grandmother sitting in a quiet and tidy house writing prose. It is our prayer that the grace we've been given will bud and flower into a harvest of grace-filled joyous children who are dazzled by God's great love for them in Christ.

Remembering God's Grace

At the end of every chapter you'll find questions that will challenge your thinking or help you clarify important principles. Please take time to work through them.

part one

Foundations
of Grace

1

From Sinai to Calvary

*The law of God, the most salutary [beneficial] doctrine of life, cannot
advance humans on their way to righteousness, but rather hinders them.*
~ **MARTIN LUTHER**[1]

Mom and her three children were all seated on the floor in the brightly
colored playroom. It was time for their Bible game. Two of the three children loved the game because they usually got all the answers right, but one,
Jordan, the middle child, was alternately sullen and disruptive.

"Who wants to draw the first card?" Mom asked.

Two hands shot up simultaneously. "I do, I do!" they both chimed.

"Okay, Joshua, you go first."

Joshua picked a card from the pile and read, "Tell the story of Jonah in
your own words and then talk about what the story means to you."

Joshua then proceeded to talk about Jonah's being commanded to serve
God but being disobedient so instead got swallowed by a whale. Afterward
the whale vomited him onto the ground (the three boys giggled), and then
Jonah obeyed.

"Good job, Joshua! Now, what does the story teach us?" Mom asked.

Caleb's hand was the first one up. "It means that we should obey when
God tells us to do something, like to go tell people about God."

"Right, Caleb! Now, can you think of some ways to tell people about
God?"

Different answers were shouted out. "We could bake cookies for our neighbors and invite them to church!" and "We could offer to do chores for them, too!"

"Yes," Mom said. "That's exactly right. Now, Jordan, can you tell me what you could do to obey God?"

Jordan stammered out a weak, "I don't know."

"Can't you think of anything at all?"

Becoming more defiant, Jordan shouted, "No, and I don't want to!"

"But, Jordan, you don't want to get swallowed by a whale, do you? God tells us to serve our neighbors and tell them about him. If you can't be good, you won't get any goldfish crackers or the blue Jell-O I've made."

Sadly, many Christian parents can relate to this painful little story. In an effort to teach our children about the Bible, we frequently employ the stories in the Bible as a way to compel obedience. Can you picture doing something like that with your kids? I know I can. In fact, it's just the way that I used the Bible when I was raising mine. I can remember a little song we sang that went something like this:

> I don't want to be a Jonah
> And get swallowed by a whale.
> So to Nineveh I will go,
> For the Lord has told me so,
> And I'll shout aloud, "You must be born again!"

I took every story in the Bible and made it about what my children were supposed to be doing. I took every story of grace and mercy (like Jonah's) and made it into law and morals: "You better obey. There are whales about!" Just like the seminary professor's pastor we learned about in the Introduction, I didn't give my kids the gospel story. I assumed that they had heard it enough times and that they had believed it. Jesus and the cross? That was old news. The real action was in obeying, not in remembering. What I didn't know then was that *the good news about Jesus's obedience and shameful death was the only motif that would grant my children a heart to obey*. So we ate goldfish and blue Jell-O, sang songs about Jonah, and worried about whales.

Right about now you might be wondering if we're saying that parents should never give their children any commands. Please don't misunderstand; we're not saying that at all. Every faithful parent *must* give their

28

children guidance, direction, rules, and commands. What we are saying is that these things are not to be the primary theme of our teaching. The primary theme is to be Jesus Christ and the work he's *already done*.

Over the next several pages you'll read about the different kinds of commands parents are to give their children, along with the kinds of obedience that these commands may produce. But for now, please stop for a moment and ask yourself what percentage of your time is spent in *declaring the rules* and what percentage in *reciting the Story*. Of course, if your children are very young, it is certainly understandable if most of your time is spent with the rules. You can't have long discussions about justification with a two-year-old. But, even so, you can begin to bring the good news about Jesus's work as soon as they are able to understand.

Now that you've thought about whether you give them more rules or gospel, you can recite the story of the Rescuer to yourself:

Your Father so loved you that he sent his Son to rescue you from the punishment that was due you for your sins. These are the sins you committed when you were a child, the sins you committed before you became a believer, and the ones you've committed today. He has seen all your sin: your selfishness, anger, laziness, and pride, and he has loved you. To rescue you, his Son was sent from heaven, his home, to be born as a human baby, live a perfect life, suffer in shame and humiliation on Calvary, rise again after three days, and then ascend to the right hand of his Father, where he watches over and redeems every facet of your life, including your parenting. He has promised to use everything in your life for your good and his glory. This is the kind of watchful, fatherly love he has for you. He is the perfect parent, and this record of perfection has been transferred to you, if you have put your trust in him. Your children's salvation doesn't depend on you any more than your own salvation did. He's a wonderful Father. You can rest in his everlasting arms—now.

One of the reasons we don't share this story with our children is that it doesn't resonate deeply in our own hearts. As one mom of four told us, "I couldn't teach my kids about the gospel before because it was not real to me and had no impact on me. Although I was a Christian, I was trying to live by the law and expecting my kids to live by it too—or else. Praise God that although I mess up every day with them, I am learning to direct them to their need for him and not their need to do good or to please me."

The following discussion about rules and obedience is obviously not everything parents should say to their kids. It is simply an introduction to the different forms of human law and obedience and a way to differentiate it from true Christian righteousness.[2]

Our Obedience and the Rules

Initial Obedience

Every responsible parent knows that there are certain things children must be taught. To begin with, our littlest kids need to know, understand, and respond immediately to the command *no*, which is why it is usually one of the first words they learn to say. They need to be taught about the words *stop* and *come to me*, for the same reasons. These words are so obviously important that they hardly need mentioning. When a child begins to dash out into a busy street, her life may depend on whether she responds to your voice. Because all responsible parents, Christian or non-Christian, teach these concepts to their children, the concepts don't have anything to do with a right standing before God, but that doesn't mean they are unimportant. These are simply concepts that will protect them from harm and enable them to begin to function within the family and society.

Social Obedience

As little ones mature, they are taught to say "Please" and "Thank you." They're taught what we would call the "social laws" of their particular culture. For instance, in some cultures, burping loudly after a meal is a sign of gratitude for good food. In American culture it is usually considered boorish. These rules or laws about polite behavior are transient from one era to another and from one country or region to another. Manners in North America's Deep South differ significantly from those in the Northeast and the Southwest. Because the Bible doesn't instruct us in good etiquette, good manners are not a matter of Christian righteousness, although that doesn't mean that we shouldn't teach them to our children.

Of course, if a child has been told not to burp at the dinner table but defiantly continues to do so, his disobedience is more than just a manners issue. It may be an issue of submission to authority, which transfers it into a higher category. If he is being willfully disobedient, it is sinful.

We will talk more about this later, but for now what we want you to remember is that the social conventions of any particular culture don't have anything to do with one's standing before a holy God. Even if little Johnny never burped at the table, it doesn't mean that he has right standing before God. It may simply mean that he has good digestion, that he can't burp on demand, or that he is a man-pleaser by nature and doesn't want to make anyone mad at him. The kingdom of God is not a matter of burping or slurping. It is righteousness, peace, and joy in the Holy Spirit (Rom. 14:17).

Civic Obedience

Children must also be taught to be law-abiding citizens. That means that they are instructed in the laws of the land in which they live and are told that they must obey them. This is another category of law that even responsible secularists teach their children. All children, believing or not, must be taught not to cheat on tests or steal. They must learn that lying has consequences and that disobeying those in authority, whether parents, teachers, or police, is unacceptable.

Wesley needed to learn that he could not beat up anyone who got in his way. This, too, is not a matter of Christian righteousness. It is simply a matter of learning how to get along with other people in a world where others have the propensity to get in your way or mess with your Thomas Trains. While it is true that you should not haul off and punch any person who displeases you, it is also true that an unregenerate pacifist will feel God's wrath in the same way that an unregenerate bully will. Of course, it's better for a family and a society to be peace loving rather than violent and abusive, but ultimately before God only Christ's righteousness will suffice.

Religious Obedience

Religious obedience is what we teach children to do as part of a life of faith before they come to faith. For instance, we ask them to wait before we eat so that we can thank God for our food. This is usually nothing more than a religious exercise for them. They learn when to stand up in church, when to sing, and when to sit quietly. They learn to give their pennies in Sunday school.

We call this form of obedience "religious obedience" because it has to do with the practices of the faith, but it is not necessarily the fruit of saving faith. It may be the fruit of any number of things, including a desire to avoid discipline or, worst of all, a desire to feel good about their own obedience. Of course, it may also be the fruit of real faith, but we must *never* assume that because a child closes his eyes when the family prays, he's regenerate. Outward conformity to religious exercises is not proof of regeneration. Jewish children are reverent during religious services, and unbelievers sit quietly during wedding ceremonies.

Training children in religious obedience is not wrong; in fact, we are commanded to do so. We are told to teach them the Bible, to talk with them about God's nature and works, to pray in their presence, and to take them to worship (see Ex. 12:26–28; Deut. 4:9–10; 6:7–9; Ps. 78:4–8; Eph. 6:4). But telling children that they are good or that God is pleased with them because they closed their eyes during prayer time is both dangerous and false. So, what should a parent say to encourage little four-year-old Benjamin, who always fidgets and causes distractions, when he is finally able to sit quietly for five minutes while the family prays? You might say something like this:

> Bennie, I'm thankful that the Lord helped you to sit quietly tonight. I know that's hard for you because you've got so many wiggles and you don't under-stand what we're doing. But on nights like tonight, when you are able to sit quietly, it's because God is helping you learn to obey. Someday you'll know how wonderful he is and how much he loves you, whether you wiggle or not. Then you'll want to talk with him, too. But for tonight I just want you to know that your quiet sitting helps me know that he's working in your heart. Now, where did those wiggles get to?

On the other hand, you might be wondering what you should say when Bennie disrupts, wiggles, and talks all during the prayer time. You might say:

> Do you know why we love to pray, Bennie? We love to pray because our hearts were just like yours. We never wanted to spend five minutes of our time talking to God. All we wanted to do was have fun, and it didn't seem like fun to talk to God. But then God changed our hearts so we could see how amazing he is. He showed us that even though we didn't love him or like to talk to him, he loved us anyway. And when you find out how kind someone has been to you and how amazing his love is for you, it makes you want to talk to him. Honestly there are still times I don't want to sit and talk to God, but even in those times he loves me just the same as the times when I love talking to him. But do you know what is more important than sitting still during prayer? Having a God that loves you no matter what—that is more

important. Understanding how your heart would be hard and disobedient all the time without his help is more important. And asking Jesus to change your heart to love him and to forgive you for not loving him is the most important thing of all.

Now, Bennie, we have talked to you previously about disrupting family prayer. I understand that your heart is not drawn to God during prayer yet. I am glad that you are not pretending to pray with us, because that would be lying. I am praying for you that God changes your heart so that you will want to pray with the family. But until that happens, we are requiring you to sit quietly during prayer time. You have become a distraction to those of us who want to pray, so I am reminding you that your continued distraction will result in discipline. [We'll talk more about discipline in chapter 6.]

There is a marked difference between this kind of gracious parenting and the moralistic parenting I did when I was raising my children. I would alternately tell them that they were good when they sat quietly or tell them that they had to close their eyes and pray or be disciplined when they were bad. My parenting had very little to do with the gospel. I assumed my children had regenerate hearts because they had prayed a prayer at some point and because I required religious obedience from them. This resulted in kids who were alternately hypocritical and rebellious. It taught them how to feign prayer, without pressing them to long for the Savior who loved hypocrites and rebels.

Religious obedience is probably the most difficult and dangerous form of obedience simply because it is so easily confused with conformity to God's law. It's the place where most Christian families go terribly wrong. Yes, we are commanded to teach the Word, prayer, and worship to our children, but their acquiescence to these things won't save them. Only the righteous life, death, and resurrection of Jesus Christ saves them.

By way of reminder then, we have demonstrated four levels of rules and corresponding obedience: basic instruction in hearing and obeying; social rules or manners; civic rules and submission to human authority; and, finally, religious training. None of these levels of obedience are meritorious. That is, none of them can *earn* approval from God. In fact, each of these different forms of obedience may actually blind a compliant child to his need for a Savior. But that's where the law of God comes in.

God's Beautiful, Holy, Good—and Crushing—Law

The apostle Paul, a Jewish rabbi who had extensive respect for and acquaintance with God's law (Acts 22:3) had some very shocking thoughts about it once he came to faith in Christ. Although he heartily agreed that it was "holy and righteous and good" (Rom. 7:12), and although he knew the beautiful nature of God's law, he also knew that the law could never bring sinners to life because *no one* could obey it. He confessed that all his obedience (and it was extensive) had no more value than a pile of manure (Phil. 3:8). He wrote:

> By works of the law no human being will be justified in his sight. (Rom. 3:20)

> What then? Are we Jews [who have the written law] any better off [than Gentiles who don't]? No, not at all. For we have already charged that all, both Jews and Greeks, are under sin, as it is written: "None is righteous, no, not one; no one understands; no one seeks for God." (Rom. 3:9–11)

> All [Jews and Gentiles] have sinned and fall short of the glory of God. (Rom. 3:23)

> The very commandment that promised life ["If you obey . . . then you shall live," Deut. 30:16] proved to be death to me [because although Paul tried, he couldn't obey it]. (Rom. 7:10)

> For all who rely on works of the law are under a curse; for it is written, "Cursed be everyone who does not abide by *all* things written in the Book of the Law, and do them." Now it is evident that no one is justified before God by the law [because our fundamental disobedience brings us under God's curse rather than under his blessing]. (Gal. 3:10–11)

> [The law is a] . . . ministry of death, carved in letters on stone. (2 Cor. 3:7)

> You are severed from Christ, you who would be justified by the law. (Gal. 5:4)

These words about God's law and our condition of lawlessness should make us stop and seriously question how we use the law in our own lives and in the lives of our children. When we seek to have right standing (justification) before a holy God through compliance to it, we are *severed, cut off,*

34

separated from the grace and righteousness provided by Jesus Christ. We are on our own. We are falling as sinners into the hands of a terrifyingly holy and all-powerful God. When we teach our children to do the same thing, we are drowning them in a "ministry of death." Why death? Because that's the inevitable result when sinners ignore Jesus Christ and seek holiness on their own.

This is serious business. It is no wonder then that the great reformer Martin Luther wrote, "The law of God, the most salutary [beneficial] doctrine of life, cannot advance humans on their way to righteousness, but rather hinders them."[3] The law of God, although beneficial and beautiful, *cannot* advance us on our way to righteousness because we *cannot obey it.* Although the law demands perfection in only two areas, none of us (reread the passages above if you need to), no, *none of us* fully complies. What are these two areas? Jesus laid them out for us in Matthew 22:36–40:

> "Teacher, which is the great commandment in the Law?" And [Jesus] said to him, "You shall love the Lord your God with all your heart and with all your soul and with all your mind. This is the great and first commandment. And a second is like it: You shall love your neighbor as yourself. On these two commandments depend all the Law and the Prophets."

Pure, unadulterated, consistent love for God and pure, unadulterated, consistent love for others is the summation of all the law God has given us in both the Old and New Testaments. Of course, the problem is that we never obey these simple commands. We always love ourselves more than we love God or others. We are always erecting idols in our hearts and worshiping and serving them. We are always more focused on what we want and how we might get it than we are on loving him and laying down our life for others. The law does show us the right way to live, but none of us obeys it. Not for one millisecond.

Even though our children cannot and will not obey God's law, we need to teach it to them again and again. And when they tell us that they can't love God or others in this way, we are not to argue with them. We are to agree with them and tell them of their need for a Savior.

The law of God also hinders our advance toward righteousness because, in our pride, we think that if we just try hard enough or repent deeply enough, we'll be able to obey it. We read the promises of life for obedience and think that means that we can do it. The promises of life for obedience are not meant to build our self-confidence. They're meant to make us long for obedience and then, when we fail *again*, they're meant to crush us and drive us to Christ.

In addition, the law defeats us by awakening the sin that is resident within us. As Paul said, "I would not have known what it is to covet if the law had not said, 'You shall not covet.' But sin, seizing an opportunity through the commandment, produced in me all kinds of covetousness" (Rom. 7:7–8). In other words, the very law that was meant to bring life stirs up a desire for sin and kills us. Again, that doesn't mean that we don't teach our children God's law. We are commanded to do so *but not to make them good*. We are commanded to give them the law so that they will be crushed by it and see their need for a Savior. The law won't make them good. *It will make them despair of ever being good enough, and in that way it will make them open to the love, sacrifice, and welcome of their Savior, Jesus Christ.*

Yes, give them God's law. Teach it to them and tell them that God commands obedience. But before you are done, give them grace and explain again the beautiful story of Christ's perfect keeping of it for them. Jesus Christ was the only one who ever deserved to hear, "You are good," but he relinquished his right relationship with the law and his Father and suffered as a lawbreaker. This is the message we all need to hear, and it is the only message that will transform our hearts.

The Gospel or Law

Everything that isn't gospel is law. Let us say it again: *everything that isn't gospel is law.* Every way we try to make our kids good that isn't rooted in the good news of the life, death, resurrection, and ascension of Jesus Christ is damnable, crushing, despair-breeding, Pharisee-producing law. We won't get the results we want from the law. We'll get either shallow self-righteousness or blazing rebellion or both (frequently from the same kid on the same day!). We'll get moralistic kids who are cold and hypocritical and who look down on others (and could easily become Mormons), or you'll get teens who are rebellious and self-indulgent and who can't wait to get out of the house. We have to remember that in the life of our unregenerate children, the law is given for one reason only: to crush their self-confidence and drive them to Christ.

The law also shows believing children what gospel-engendered gratitude looks like. But one thing is for sure: we aren't to give our children the law to make them good. It won't, because it can't. In our hearts we know that's true because the law hasn't made us good, either, has it?

Oh, you remember that little game we described at the beginning of the chapter? The idea for it is from MormonChic.com, a website written by Mormons for Mormons. If a Mormon can play the game exactly the same way you do, it isn't a Christian game.[4] It's a morality game and we aren't moralists; we're Christians. If a Mormon can parent the same way you do, your parenting isn't Christian.

Now, how would that game have been different if we remembered that every story is about God's grace through Jesus Christ and the gospel? After Joshua recited the bare facts of the story, his mother would have drawn out the story's real meaning. The story of Jonah isn't about learning to be obedient or facing the consequences. The story of Jonah is about how God is merciful to both the religiously self-righteous, unloving Pharisee (Jonah) and the irreligious, violent pagan. The story is a story about God's ability to save souls and use us even when we disobey. It's a story about God's mercy, not our obedience. Here's how the conversation would differ if we were giving gospel instead of law:

"Good job, Joshua! Now what does the story teach us?" Mom asked.

Caleb's hand was the first one up. "It means that we should obey when God tells us to do something, like go tell people about God."

"Yes, Caleb, we are to obey God, but that's not the primary message of the story. Can you think of any other message?"

Jordan piped up. "Lots of times people don't want to obey God."

"Right, Jordan! That's exactly right. I know that it's hard for me to obey. I'm just like Jonah, too.

"Can you think of any other messages? No? Then let me help you. This story is a message about how kind and merciful God is. He was kind to the bad people from Nineveh because he didn't destroy them even though they deserved it. He was kind to them by making them believe the message that Jonah told them. But he was also kind to Jonah. Even though Jonah didn't love his neighbors (the people from Nineveh), God didn't leave him to die in the belly of a big fish, although that was what he deserved. Instead he gave him another chance and kept giving him chances even though Jonah didn't really love God or his merciful nature. God gives us so many opportunities to obey him because he loves us and is so merciful. God shows us how he loves us because his dear Son, Jesus, spent three days in a very dark place just like Jonah did. He spent three days in a grave after dying for our sins. But then he rose again from the dead so that we could be good in God's eyes and tell other people about how loving he is. Can you think of some things we could do so that other people would know about God's love?"

Different answers were shouted out. "We could bake cookies for our neighbors and invite them to church!" and "We could offer to do chores for them, too!"

"Right! Now let's celebrate God's mercy and have a party with some goldfish crackers and blue Jell-O I've made."[5]

Remembering God's Grace

Please don't ignore what the Holy Spirit might be doing in your heart through this chapter. Please do take the time to think deeply about it and answer the following questions.

1) In what ways do you use the Bible as a rule book instead of as the "good news"?
2) Does your love of the gospel change the way you parent? If not, how could it?
3) What are the four categories of obedience outlined in this chapter? Have you used these different categories to make your children think they can earn God's favor?
4) Why is it important for parents and children to learn the proper place of the law?
5) How does a full view of grace change the way we teach the law?
6) Summarize what you've learned in this chapter in three or four sentences.

2

How to Raise Good Kids

Faith is the complete fulfilling of the law, and will fill those who believe with such righteousness that they will need nothing else for justification.
~ MARTIN LUTHER[1]

Into the nothingness and vacuity of the formless void, the Creative Word spoke. "Let there be light!" and light burst forth. Iridescent colors danced into the universe. Shimmering prisms of living light suffused splendor into the air. The Father, Son, and Spirit rejoiced in what they saw. The Creative Word smiled. He declared, "You're Good!"[2]

Day after day the depth and complexity of his work multiplied as God filled emptiness with glory. Light and darkness, heaven and earth, seas and land, plants and trees, and stars and moons—all beloved, all beautiful, all good. Fish and birds swarmed and flocked. Eagles and parrots, great sea creatures, and tiny krill entered into God's joy in himself and his creation. It was a thundering, harmonious hymn in celebration of life, wisdom, power, and goodness. Livestock and creeping things and beasts of the earth sprang into being at the sound of his voice. "You are good! Live! Be fruitful! Multiply! Rejoice!" In pure bliss they dashed to do his bidding, each singing with unique voice.

Then, finally, on the sixth day all was in readiness. God's beautiful new home was decorated and replete with an excess of splendor, provision, goodness. The grand celebration was about to begin, and it was time for the honored guests to arrive. He took into his hand some of the ground he had made. He fashioned it with care and breathed into it his "breath of life."

He spoke to it, "Image me! You are my mirror. You, above all else that I have made, will display my goodness."

Adam (and later Eve) breathed in, and, very likely, the first thing they saw was the living Word. He smiled at his children. "I have created you to be like me, and so you are. You will love and desire goodness because I am good and have made you good. This earth is yours. Guard it, tend it, fill it with millions who are good like me. Now sing with me and rejoice, for I have made you to know me and to love me. You are blessed above all that I have created."

Then God looked over his creation. Like a lordly host at a long-anticipated reception, he pondered all he had made. He declared: "You are very good!" At his word, choirs in the heavens and on the earth filled the earth with the majestic melody, harmony, and rhythm. The morning stars sang, the trees of the fields clapped their hands, the mountains bowed low in worship. "The Lord is good and he has made us good! Hurray for our good God! Hurray for his good creation!"

The End of Our Goodness—for Now

Then, in one fell swoop, the lie was believed, the goodness was doubted, and all was lost. Rather than celebrating the goodness it had been given, all there is was subjected to futility, bondage, and decay, and relentless, painful groaning (Rom. 8:20, 22). Misery, suspicion, sickness, wandering, and destitution of heart replaced the majestic music and celebration. The light turned to shadow. Death filled God's beautiful home so that it was no longer wholly good. It had fallen; evil infected all he had made. In place of the Lord's benediction and approval, wrath and the curse would reign.

Banished from their home, the shattered mirrors became strangers, isolated from one another and their God. The desperate search to regain goodness had begun. Their anguished, futile efforts at goodness would supplant the joyful benediction, "You are good!" So, in desperation to hear it once again, they sought ways to bestow it upon themselves. In furious envy their firstborn son would murder his younger brother because he did not attain it, while his brother did. *Is Abel's offering good and mine bad? Fine, I'll just kill him since you think he's so great!*

This isn't merely ancient history. The apostle John warns us today, "We should not be like Cain, who was of the evil one and murdered his brother.

40

And why did he murder him? *Because his own deeds were evil and his brother's righteous*" (1 John 3:12). Cain idolized God's approval and in furious envy chose murder as the way he would deal with the one who had attained it. His descendants would create pejorative names for those who worked hard to hear it most: "holier-than-thou," "self-righteous prig," "goodie-two-shoes." His descendants would emulate them or murder them in their hearts (Matt. 5:21) to silence the voice of the guilt that nagged them.

In an effort to prove that they no longer needed God's help to be good, the men from Babel rose up to build a tower to their own honor and bestowed the benediction upon themselves. "Wow! Look at that!" they said. "We're great! We're good!" Rather than telling them that their efforts were a nice try, God cursed them with confusion of speech, and they wandered apart too. This is our history, the legacy of every person who ever drew breath and tried to prove that he really was okay. Every person but One.

How would God respond to such wickedness? In righteous justice, he could have wiped us all out or simply left us to degenerate back into the dust from which he created us. But he didn't. Instead he sent goodness back into his world. Goodness was born as a baby in Bethlehem, and we did what we always do with goodness: we tried to slaughter it. Then he burst onto the Judean landscape, and while he was reestablishing our righteousness in the River Jordan, the earth once again heard the blessed benediction.

[Jesus said] . . . "It is fitting for us to fulfill all righteousness." . . . And when Jesus was baptized, immediately he went up from the water, and behold, the heavens were opened to him, and he saw the Spirit of God descending like a dove and coming to rest on him; and behold, a voice from heaven said, "*This is my beloved Son, with whom I am well pleased.*" (Matt. 3:15–17)

Jesus had come to fulfill all goodness and righteousness. Where we had failed, he would succeed. He would be circumcised for us, baptized for us. He would respond to his parents' unjust questioning of his goodness with righteousness and truth. He would love his Father and his neighbor perfectly, and then he would be stripped of all the reward for the goodness he had earned. He would be called a demon-possessed blasphemer. He would be smitten for saying he was God. He wouldn't hear "Good job!" He would hear deafening silence. He would receive the curse of God's abandonment.

And, like Cain before us, we would kill him in the name of goodness to rid our world of such audacity.

But Jesus wouldn't idolize God's approval; instead he would worship God and love us. He was goodness personified. Then, to vindicate him and prove that God's benediction rested upon him, God would raise him from the dead. In an outrageous demonstration of the Father's love of goodness and his love for us, he would transfer all Jesus's goodness to us—if we would believe that he is that wise, loving, and good.

Lie to Your Child to Make Him Good

So much of what we're advised to do as parents is so that our kids will feel good about themselves. This advice has roots in the self-esteem movement, which claimed that a child's success in life is based on whether or not he feels that he is good. Although the modern self-esteem movement began in the 1950s and 1960s, this was no novel lie. It has been around for thousands of years. It's the same deception that Eve believed in the beginning. *Yum,* she thought; *this fruit looks good and it will make me good. I think we'll have it for dinner tonight.* Since the fall of the human race, we've been alternately telling ourselves that we are good, that if we try hard enough we'll be good enough, or that being good is an impossibility so we should just give up and have fun. After all, nobody's perfect!

In light of all this, what are we parents to do? If you believe the Bible, we are sure you realize that neither we nor our children are truly good. "Good girl!" "Good job!" "You're a beautiful princess!"—that is the unceasing refrain as parents seek to create their version of successful, good children. But when all the other parents in the play-group spend the day telling little Rebekah how good she is, how are Christian parents to respond? Rather than telling Rebekah that she's a good girl, we could say, "I noticed you shared your swing. Do you know what that reminds me of? How Christ shared his life with us. I'm so thankful for God's working in your life that way. I know that neither of us would ever do anything kind if God wasn't helping us. I'm so thankful."

In case you're wondering if the Bible gives an example of this kind of encouragement, here is Luke's report of what happened when Barnabas saw the grace of God working in the people of Antioch: "They sent Barnabas to Antioch. When he came and saw the grace of God, he was glad, and he exhorted them all to remain faithful to the Lord with steadfast purpose" (Acts 11:22–23). Barnabas saw God's grace working in the lives of the people, so he exhorted them to remain faithful. We too can see God's grace at work in our children and exhort them to remain faithful.

Let's say that Rebekah has a habit of selfishness, so before Mom drives her to her play date, they spend some time praying together. Mom could simply thank God for sharing so much good—such as friends, sunshine, play dates—with Rebekah and then ask him to help her remember his generosity when others want what she is using. Then, if Mom notices her sharing, she can say, "Rebekah, you're sharing! Isn't it great to see how God answered our prayer? You see, Rebekah, even though we all hate to share, God is more powerful than our selfishness. Isn't he good?"

Because we wonder whether Rebekah is regenerate, we won't thank her for obeying God's law. If she isn't saved, she doesn't have the Holy Spirit, and she cannot choose to respond to God or obey his law from the heart. The one encouragement we can always give our children (and one another) is that God is more powerful than our sin, and he's strong enough to make us want to do the right thing. We can assure them that his help can reach everyone, even them. Our encouragement should always stimulate praise for God's grace rather than for our goodness.

On the other hand, if we persist in seeking to build our children's self-esteem by praising them, we make them into our own image, boys and girls who *idolize the benediction*, adults who are enslaved to the opinions of others, and parents who pass on the lie to the next generation—even though it hasn't worked to make them good either. Like us, our children crave the blessed benediction: "You are good!" But the Bible says that because we are not good, those words no longer apply to us. We're not good. Here's how the Bible describes our plight: "The Lord saw that the wickedness of man was great in the earth, and that *every intention of the thoughts of his heart was only evil continually*" (Gen. 6:5).

We long to be told, "You are good!" but only Jesus Christ and those clothed in his goodness deserve to hear it. And if we really embrace this truth, our parenting will be transformed from wishful deception to powerful grace. It will make our parenting Christian. Our children aren't innately good, and we shouldn't tell them that they are. But they are loved and if they truly believe that, his love will transform them.

Human Obedience and Christian Righteousness

In the last chapter we discussed four levels of human law and the resulting kinds of obedience we might expect from our children. We talked about initial, social, civic, and religious law and obedience. These four levels are what we call "human obedience."

Diagram 2.1: Human Obedience

Initial obedience: learning to obey Dad's and Mom's voices
Social obedience: learning the social codes of society
Civic obedience: learning to obey the laws of society
Religious obedience: learning the religious practices of family and church

As you can see, what we're calling "human obedience" is the sort of obedience that is generally good for our family and society. Human obedience encompasses the entire breadth of human goodness. This obedience or outward goodness is achievable by every person, saved or unsaved, because of God's common grace.[3] In some ways, society is certainly better off if people observe social, civic, and religious laws, if people try to be good to each other. It is more advantageous to live in a land of peace and freedom than of strife and slavery (Titus 3:1–2). Respect, courtesy, and civil obedience are blessings from the Lord, who bestows his blessings on the just and the unjust (Matt. 5:45).

But if our human obedience or morality isn't motivated by gratitude for God's grace, it is very dangerous. If not rooted in gratitude for God's love for us in Christ, morality is deadlier to the soul than immorality. Why? Remember that Jesus said it is those who are lost, who know they need a physician, that he came to save (Luke 19:10). Those who excel at the sort of obedience listed above may not see their need for a Savior; their hearts may be hardened and unfazed by God's grace. Remember that it was the woman who knew that she had been forgiven for much who loved much (Luke 7:47). Forgiveness for deep offenses breeds deep love. Forgiveness for perceived and reasonable slights breeds apathetic disdain. A society riddled with immorality will not be a pleasant place to live, but a society riddled with self-congratulatory morality will be satanic and resistant to grace. It will be nice and tidy and loveless and, oh, so dead. And it will be only a breath away from murder. Remember that it was the religious leaders, not the prostitutes, who called for the execution of the Christ.

Teaching our children to be well-behaved, good citizens is proper as far as it goes. But we must never mistake this training for Christian nurture or discipline, nor should we mistake their acquiescence to our social mores as true Christian righteousness. Just to be sure that you understand what we mean when we use the phrase "Christian righteousness," let us define it here for you: *Christian righteousness is that level of goodness that can withstand the scrutiny of a perfectly holy God and earn the benediction, "You are good!"* It is perfect obedience in both outward conformity and inward desire. It is goodness for the sake of God's great glory motivated by a pure and zealous love for God and neighbor. It is the right action at the right time for the right reason. A record of this kind of goodness can never be earned; it can only be bestowed by grace through faith.

A Goodness Bestowed

Christian righteousness differs from the kinds of obedience that we are used to teaching our kids. It is a goodness given to us by God out of his sheer generosity and mercy and rests squarely on the obedience and sacrifice of Jesus Christ alone. Christians have been teaching their children about this Christian righteousness for centuries. Some have taught their children about it by asking and answering key questions. Here's one of those questions and answers about Christian righteousness:

Q. How are you right with God?

A. Only by true faith in Jesus Christ. Even though my conscience accuses me of having grievously sinned against all God's commandments and of never having kept any of them, and even though I am still inclined toward all evil, nevertheless, without my deserving it at all, out of sheer grace, God grants and credits to me the perfect satisfaction, righteousness, and holiness of Christ as if I had never sinned or been a sinner, as if I had been as perfectly obedient as Christ was obedient for me. All I need to do is to accept this gift of God with a believing heart.[4]

Christian righteousness is different from human obedience because it is granted to us by God's grace, not because of our works or our children's merit. It is not something we can earn, but rather it is a gift we are given, even though we continue to sin terribly. The righteousness we are given is the very record of the righteousness of Jesus Christ. When we have Christian righteousness, God looks upon us and our believing children as being perfectly obedient, no matter how we fail. God doesn't smile at us one day and frown when we blow it the next. When our children have been given the gift of Christian righteousness, God is *always* smiling at them because he sees them in his Son.

The way we receive this righteousness is by believing that God is good enough to give it to us and telling him that we want it more than we want our self-generated goodness. The diagram below will help you understand the differences between human obedience and passive (what is done for us) righteousness.

Diagram 2.2: Human Obedience and Passive Righteousness

Human Obedience	Passive Righteousness
Accessible to all who work	Accessible only to those who believe
Outward conformity to rules and law	Record of Christ's obedience is bestowed upon all who believe
Renewed by self-effort and resolutions	Initiated and renewed by the Holy Spirit
Temporary and fluctuating	Eternal and settled
Imperfect and incomplete	Perfect and complete
Grinding slavery of works	Grateful obedience of faith
Produces fear and insecurity	Produces peace and godly confidence
Results in pride and despair	Results in rest and joy

This Christian righteousness is sometimes called "justification." *Justification* is a word that simply means that our record is both "just as if we had never sinned" and also "just as if we had always obeyed." A justified child or adult has a record of perfect obedience in God's eyes because the obedience of the perfect Son has been transferred to him by faith. Justified Christians are perfectly forgiven *and* perfectly righteous. When God looks at the justified believer, parent or child, he sees us not only as forgiven (which is great news) but also as obedient and righteous (which ought to amaze and astound us). If Christian righteousness or *justification* is new to you, here are a few verses that demonstrate it:

For we hold that one is *justified by faith apart from works of the law*. (Rom. 3:28)

Yet we know that a person is *not justified by works of the law but through faith in Jesus Christ*, so we also have believed in Christ Jesus, *in order to be justified by faith in Christ and not by works of the law, because by works of the law no one will be justified*. (Gal. 2:16)

Now before faith came, we were held captive under the law, imprisoned until the coming faith would be revealed. So then, the law was our guardian until Christ came, in order that we might be *justified by faith*. (Gal. 3:23–24)

In summary then, this is what we have learned about our goodness: in the beginning, God declared that everything he had made (including Adam and Eve) was good. This benediction of goodness filled the hearts of all his creatures and they rejoiced in him. Then sin entered and our ability to attain true goodness was lost. Immediately people began to try to find goodness on their own. Eventually those who strove to be very good killed the only truly good Man who ever lived. But even through this murderous act, God's perfect will was accomplished so that all who would believe would receive both forgiveness and righteousness.[5]

"Kids, Go Put Away Your Goodness!"

Right about now you might be wondering why we've strayed so far from the usual fare found in parenting books. We're talking about the difference between obedience and righteousness because these categories make up the primary curriculum of what we teach our children every day. Every word we say to them during the day will be shaped by our view of their ability to be good and how to get them there. Every responsible parent wants obedient children. But if we're confused about their ability to be good, we'll end up lying to them about their desperate lostness outside of Christ. We'll tell them they are good and that they can obey God's law.

Even though our dismal lack of goodness (yes, even in our parenting) has been demonstrated for thousands of years, we still strive for our own goodness and train our children to do the same. We make charts for our children and give them stickers that proclaim "You're Great!" We plaster our cars with bumper stickers that announce that our kids are the best citizen in their class (even though all children in the class get a sticker in order to protect their fragile self-esteem). We tell them that making mommy or daddy happy by being good is the goal of life, thereby turning them into people who are enslaved to the opinions and approval of others and always hungering for more. And we instill within them the drive to prove themselves better than others, whether that's through being very good or being very bad.

Better Than Charts and Stickers

Tell your children every day what God requires from them, and when they groan under the weight of it, give them this invitation: "Oh, taste and see that the LORD is good! Blessed is the [boy or girl] who takes refuge in him!" (Ps. 34:8).

Keep displaying his goodness to them. Do it over and over and over again. Because we don't know the state of our children's souls and because they might simply want to please us by praying to be saved, we must continue to give them the law and encourage them to ask God for faith to believe that he is as good as he says he is. Perhaps they are truly saved, and, if so, the law will help them learn what real goodness looks like. Remember, *their obedience does not make them righteous*, but if they are righteous, if they've tasted how good he is, then they will begin to desire to obey out of a heart of gratitude. If a child is regenerate, he will grow in his desire to know and to demonstrate his love for God.

We will also give God's law to our children who say they are saved to make them thankful for Christ's perfect keeping of it in their place. When they fail to obey, they can thank God that their relationship with him isn't predicated upon their obedience but upon Jesus' obedience. Even their disobedience can be an occasion to remind them that their Savior is praying for them and that their sin won't ever separate them from him or his love for them. He continues to smile at them because they are his beloved children, with whom he is well pleased. You can continue to assure them that they are finally and fully good because of what he's done—if they are truly his.

When a child who claims to be saved obeys (albeit not perfectly) he can thank God that he was able to do so only because Jesus has given him his

Holy Spirit. In this way he can be taught to see that both his obedience *and* his disobedience are occasions for thankfulness to God.[6]

Jesus's Righteousness Establishes Our Goodness

Let's revisit that colorful playroom again. Today, instead of learning about Jonah, we're studying the Ten Commandments. The lesson called for making two tablets that look like the stone tablets that God wrote his perfect law upon (see Exodus 20). Cardboard, foil, scissors, and a Sharpie pen are used to illustrate the demands of God's beautiful law.

Joshua, Jordan, and Caleb are instructed to consider every one of the laws and rehearse how they have failed to obey. They then take the permanent marker and write their name by each commandment. Then they look at the blessings and curses for obedience and disobedience from Deuteronomy 28 and 29. Mom then tells them, "God demands perfect obedience to his law, children, but that's not all he's done. Let me read you something else that is so exciting out of the Bible:"

> When you were stuck in your old sin-dead life, you were incapable of responding to God. God brought you alive—right along with Christ! Think of it! All sins forgiven, the slate wiped clean, that old arrest warrant canceled and nailed to Christ's cross. (Col. 2:13–14 MESSAGE)

Mom continues, "When we look at those ten commandments, it is obvious that we have a record of doing wrong. We are dead in our trespasses and sins. We are not good. But this verse tells us that this record of wrongdoing was nailed to the cross when Christ died, if we believe in him."

Leaving the playroom, the family then goes outside. Each of the children picks up a wooden cross made by their dad and, using a hammer and nails, covers their record of their disobedience with the wooden cross.

Mom says, "Please understand that your record of disobedience is only covered up by the cross if you have trusted in Jesus as your Rescuer. If you know that you cannot obey these commandments, no matter how hard you try, and if you know that you need someone to obey them for you, Jesus Christ is that Somebody. He is your obedience. The Bible says he is your righteousness." Here, Mom reads aloud 1 Corinthians 1:30.

She continues, "He makes you truly good inside and out. And he makes you want to obey. But if you don't care about the commandments or if you're still trying to prove that you're good enough to obey them and make God love you, you're on your own. This terrible debt of disobedience is all that you have to offer to the holy Creator of everything. So, let's pray that God opens your eyes to his law and his good news and that he turns your heart to him."

Raising good kids is utterly impossible unless they are drawn by the Holy Spirit to put their faith in the goodness of another. You cannot raise good kids, because you're not a good parent. There is only one good Parent, and he had one good Son. Together, this Father and Son accomplished everything that needed to be done to rescue us and our children from certain destruction. When we put our faith in him, he bestows the benediction upon us: "These are My beloved children, with whom I am well pleased" (see Matt. 3:17).

Give this grace to your children: tell them who they really are, tell them what they need to do, and then tell them to taste and see that the Lord is good. Give this grace to yourself, too.

Remembering God's Grace

Please don't ignore what the Holy Spirit might be doing in your heart through this chapter. Please do, take the time to think deeply about it and answer the following questions.

1) What is the history of mankind's goodness and our attempts to be good?
2) How can we encourage our kids when they are obedient? Do our words really make a difference? How?
3) What should motivate our obedience and that of our children?
4) In what ways are human obedience and passive righteousness different? In what ways do we try to make them the same?
5) How does teaching our children about justification and Christ's righteousness help them?
6) Where can parents and children find ultimate rest and hope in?
7) Summarize what you have learned in this chapter in three or four sentences.

3

This Is the Work of God

The law says, "do this," and it is never done. Grace says, "believe in this,"
and everything is already done.
~ MARTIN LUTHER[1]

Our family has annual passes to the Disneyland and California Adventure theme parks, so we happily make the drive up the I-5 several times during the year to spend the day screaming and laughing and racing from ride to ride. One of the rides that terrifies us most is Mickey's Fun Wheel, a 150-foot-tall Ferris wheel. Now, before you roll your eyes and say, "What a bunch of sissies! Scared of a Ferris wheel!" let us tell you a little more. Like most Ferris wheels, you enter a gondola or cage at the bottom of the wheel (while other people are screaming in terror at the top). Then you're lifted up, and the real "fun" begins. You see, Mickey's Fun Wheel is actually a ride within a ride. As the cages (and you) are raised by the wheel, they also slide along interior curves so that, as the wheel turns, you have the terrifying sensation that you're about to plummet 150 feet down onto the boardwalk below. And, of course, we always have children with us (some older than others) who think it's hysterical to rock the cage as much as they possibly can.

Really, we ride roller coasters and The Tower of Terror, and nothing frightens us like this thing. We've concluded that it's so frightening because we can't see where we're going and there is nothing to hang on to. No buckles. No nicely padded harnesses. It's just you and a cage gliding in some unknown pattern 150 feet over Anaheim. We're up there, flapping in the breeze and hoping that whoever welded our gondola wasn't busy texting his girlfriend when the critical welds were being made.

So far we've given you a paradigm for parenting that might feel a bit like Mickey's Fun Wheel. Or maybe it's not that much fun. We can imagine that right about now, your head might be spinning. You might be thinking that we've taken all this gospel stuff a bit too far, or you may simply be befuddled and wondering what you're supposed to do now. *Okay, I'll throw away my charts and stickers, but then what? There better be something else for me to hang on to!*

We understand. We understand because we're right there with you, swaying in that gondola with nothing under us but grace. And while we long to be free from the tyrannical misconception that our children's success is entirely up to us, our palms are beginning to get clammy, too. Like you, we're very comfortable relying on the law as the means to achieve our goals. Here's the formula we're most at ease with: *Good parenting in, good children out.* Seems easy and comforting, doesn't it? Of course, there's always the question of whether our parenting will be good enough, but still, our reliance on the law is like standing with feet firmly planted on good old terra firma. Until, of course, we remember that this is Southern California, after all.

Releasing our hold on the law causes us to feel lost and abandoned. No, of course we don't like the law, but grace is just terrifying, like swinging in that wretched gondola or free falling into faith. Trust that God is that good? Give up trust in ourselves and our own efforts?

Salvation Is of the Lord

We know you want steps and buckles and padded harnesses. We do too. And it's for this reason that we're going to remind you once again of what we wrote in the Introduction. We told you that parenting with grace must not be employed as another formula to try to control God and your children. Sure, there are plenty of practical steps you can take with your kids, but fundamentally you'll have to embrace the truth that their salvation is all of grace.

Here are a couple of examples of God's grace at work. All through this book I have confessed how moralistic our parenting style was. We rarely gave our kids the gospel. We were frequently harsh and overly strict. At other times we were apathetic and self-absorbed. Even so, here I am, writing a book on gospel parenting with our daughter, Jessica. There's a lesson in this admission. Salvation is all of grace. Please don't think that I'm being modest or humble. I'm not. Our parenting was completely law-fear-control driven. Sure, we had fun and we loved each other, but Jesus was nowhere to be found.

In addition, my own childhood was far from ideal. Although my mother loved my brother and me, she was a single parent trying to provide for us. At times she worked two jobs to try to make ends meet. My brother and I were basically left to raise ourselves alone. During our teen years my mother also struggled with a debilitating bone disorder that made her even less available to us. We never had family devotions. We never prayed before meals. Unless my grandmother took me to church, we rarely went. Because she was working, my mother rarely attended any special school function. As I grew, I became an angry, selfish, shameless unbeliever. But God saved me. He used all the heartache to make me see how great he was and how I needed him. He transformed my heart and made me love him. And he continues to use all the trouble from my childhood to make me thankful for grace.

God has been kind to Phil and me by granting us loving, Christian children, and, of course, his kindness would never mean that anyone should cavalierly ignore parenting responsibilities and assume that God will just save our kids if he wants to. No, to live like that would be unbelief, disobedience, and presumption. It would be to fail to love our children and the Lord. We are always to do our best, striving to be obedient and to love, nurture, and discipline them. But we are to do it with faith in the Lord's ability to transform hearts, not in our ability to be consistent or faithful. Seeking to be faithfully obedient parents is our responsibility; granting faith to our children is his. Freedom to love and enjoy our children flows out of the knowledge that God saves them *in spite of our best efforts*, not because of them. Salvation is of the Lord.

So then, you might ask yourself, *Well, if that's the truth, why on earth am I working so hard at this? If God really is sovereign and is going to do what he wants to do and save my children with or without me, then why am I beating my brains out? Why am I not on a cruise somewhere while a nanny cares for them?*

We understand. When confronted with God's merciful sovereignty, a sovereignty that will use both faithful and wicked parenting as the means to draw children to himself, the propensity to give up in apathy is very strong. We pride ourselves in being self-reliant. We want to work and get paid a guaranteed wage. So when we're not promised a guaranteed wage, we think we shouldn't work. This thinking is fallacious, because the relationship we have with God isn't one between a master and slave or employer and employee. It's a relationship between a loving Father and his dearly loved sons and daughters. We're not working because we want to earn a wage. We don't work to earn God's blessing. *We work because we already have it* (Rom. 4:4–8).

We work because we love him and all he's done for us. We work because he's commanded us to work. And we work because he may use our efforts at parenting as the means to draw our children to him. But we are never to work because we think our work will ultimately transform our children. Our works are never good enough or powerful enough to transform any human heart.

How can we tell whether our efforts at parenting are motivated by reliance on God's grace or on self-trust? How can we know whether we're trying to obligate God or serve him in gratitude? One way to judge is to consider your reaction when your children fail. If you are angry, frustrated, or despairing because you work so hard and they aren't responding, then you're working (at least in part) for the wrong reasons. Conversely, if you're proud when your children obey and you get those desired kudos—*Oh! your kids are so good!*—you should suspect your motives. Both pride and despair grow in the self-reliant heart.

It's Not All Up to You

So many of the dads and moms we know would characterize their parenting as hard, grinding labor. If you believe the parental angst and fatigue you feel is yours alone, consider this: In a survey conducted by Focus on the Family, the most frequent comment from mothers was that they felt like failures.[2]

Yes, of course faithful parenting is hard work. That's not what we're concerned about. We're concerned about parents who carry on their shoulders the entire burden for their kids' salvation and lifelong happiness. We were never meant to carry the ultimate responsibility for anyone's soul: neither our own nor our children's. Only the Good Shepherd is strong enough to carry a soul—that's his job, not ours. And although this kind of committed parenting appears godly, it is nothing less than works righteousness and idolatry.

Works Righteousness

Works righteousness is a deadly and false variation of godly obedience. Godly obedience is motivated by love for God and trust in his gracious plan and power. Works righteousness is motivated by unbelief; it is a reliance on our abilities and a desire to control outcomes. Works righteousness eventuates in penance: *I'll make it up to you by redoubling my efforts tomorrow!* rather than repentance: *Lord forgive me for my sin today. Thank you that you love me in spite of all my failures.* In parenting, works righteousness will cause us to be both fearful and demanding. When we see our failures, we will be overcome with fear: *I really blew it with my kids today. I'm so afraid that I'm going to ruin them!* When we see their failures, we'll be overly demanding: *I've already told you what I want you to do. Didn't you hear me? I must have told you fifty times in the last five minutes. I'm sick to death of your terrible attitude. You need to listen to me and do what I say without any complaints or grunts or eye rolls. Just do it!* It's obvious how both responses feed off each other in a never-ending cycle of anger and despair and penance.

Works righteousness obliterates the sweet comforts of grace because it cuts us off from God, who *alone* is the giver of grace. It cuts us off because he absolutely insists on being our sole Savior. This is his claim: "I, I am the Lord, and besides me *there is no savior*" (Isa. 43:11; see also 45:21). We are not nor can we be the saviors of our children. He is the Savior. When we forget this, our parenting will be pockmarked by fear, severity, and exhaustion.

On the other hand, when we rest in his gracious work we will experience the comforts he has provided for us. He delights in being worshiped as the One who "richly provides us with everything to enjoy" (1 Tim. 6:17). He loves flooding our consciences with the peace that comes from knowing our sins are forgiven and our standing before him is completely secure. When we're quietly resting in grace, we'll have grace to give our children, too. When we're freed from the ultimate responsibility of being their savior, we'll find our parenting burden becoming easy and light.

Come to me, all who labor and are heavy laden, and I will give you rest. Take my yoke upon you, and learn from me, for I am gentle and lowly in heart, and you will find rest for your souls. For my yoke is easy, and my burden is light. (Matt. 11:28–30)

Idolatry

Simply speaking, idolatry is the worship and service of any god but God. We all struggle with idolatry. In fact, it was once said that our hearts "manufacture" idols.

Within the heart of the Christian, idolatry is frequently the worship of some good, like having believing, obedient children. This desire is not sinful or idolatrous in itself; it is good. But it becomes idolatrous when we orient our entire life around it or we sin because we want it so much. When we so desperately want our children to be good that we're alternately angry, fearful, proud, or sullen, then our desire for their transformation has become the god we serve.

Yes, God does command us to train our children, but care needs to be taken that this training doesn't morph into something more important to us than God himself. Remember that Abraham was commended by God for being willing to sacrifice his son in worship to him (Gen. 22:15). Jesus also echoed this same truth when he uttered this shocking statement: "If anyone comes to me and does not *hate* his own father and mother and wife and *children* and brothers and sisters, yes, and even his own life, he cannot be my disciple" (Luke 14:26).

Idolatry is always subject to the law of diminishing returns, too. In other words, Johnnie's obedience today is never quite good enough tomorrow. I've counseled with parents whose children were godly and faithful, but these parents were dissatisfied because the children didn't live up to the parents' preconceived notions of what their children should be. If you've ever wondered why you seem to be so demanding and why "good" is never "good enough" for you, perhaps idolatry is the answer. Perhaps you once heard that successful parenting means that your children will always obey the first time they are told and with a smiling face. As with every other form of idolatry, we parents perform the prescribed rituals and expect the desired results. *Good parenting in, good kids out.* But then, when our children refuse to satisfy our desires, we feel devastated. *But I worked so hard and tried to do everything right! What happened?*

Our idolatry is a symptom of a deeper problem: unbelief. We raise our kids' success and our parenting techniques to the status of godhood because of our unbelief. We simply don't believe that God is good enough to entrust with our children's souls or that he's wise enough to know what will make us ultimately happy and satisfied. *We have far too high a view of our ability to shape our children and far too low a view of God's love and trustworthiness.* So we multiply techniques and try to control the outcome. We subconsciously hope that by our "righteousness," we will obligate God to make everything turn out the way we want. Honestly, it's no wonder that all the women sitting around the park with their kids need a nap so badly. Idolatry, like all sin, is devastating to the soul. It cuts us off from the comforts of grace, the peace of conscience, and the joy that is to be our strength.

Grace for the Meltdown

One day, when Wesley was four or so, Jessica remembers sitting in the park with a new friend we'll call Catherine. Catherine was new to Christianity and new to our church. Like all moms do at parks, she and Jessica began a conversation about raising their children. The conversation turned to the subject of discipline. Jessica was trying to biblically explain to Catherine how important consistent, loving discipline is. She talked glowingly about how beneficial it had been in little Wesley's life.

But then, when it was time to leave, Wesley decided he didn't want to go. Apparently, it was against his plan for eternal happiness. So he threw himself to the ground in the parking lot and had a fit. Jessica felt humiliated. Everything she had just said to Catherine about the benefits of discipline was flying right back in her face.

Jessica struggled with her own works righteousness. She felt fearful and angry. She struggled with her desire that her new friend think well of her and her parenting methods. She wondered, *What does she think of me now? What does she think of my son?* She started making excuses, "He normally doesn't act that way." By the time she got Wesley buckled in the car, she was consumed with her own failure as a parent. *I do exactly what the Bible says. Why isn't God helping me or changing my child? I'll never talk about parenting to anyone ever again!*

If Jessica had remembered to parent in light of grace, she could have responded differently. Knowing the character of her heavenly Father, she could have remembered that every time something unexpected happens, it is God once again approaching her in love to show her the glories of the gospel and the beauties of grace. She could have been reminded that spanking doesn't transform the soul; only Jesus Christ does. When she saw Wesley lying there throwing a fit, she could have seen a picture of her own heart. She could have heard the Lord remind her that this heart of a rebel is just like her own. The Lord might have spoken to her heart like this:

> This is you. This is what your heart is like outside of my grace. You're no different. This is just another opportunity for you to delight in my goodness to you. Do you see how angry you are? Do you see how you need me? You're ashamed because Wesley acted this way in front of a friend you were hoping to impress. But my Son is not ashamed to call you sister [Heb. 2:11]. You're focused on your reputation, because you think that friendship with Catherine will make you happy. You're forgetting that I am the source of your happiness. Wesley is helping me show you how much you need a Savior, too. You and Wesley are just alike. You're both sinful, but you're both loved. Neither one of you deserves my love but I've graciously bestowed it upon you.

Then, without idolatry, works righteousness, or unbelief, Jessica could discipline Wesley with these words:

> Sweetheart, I will discipline you now because I love you, and you must learn to control yourself. When I tell you that it is time to go, we must leave. I know you didn't want to go, but when we don't get what we want, it isn't okay to start screaming and throw yourself to the ground. There are two things you must understand: first, you were being unsafe. God has put me in charge of you, and he has told me to keep you safe. When you lie in a parking lot with cars around, you could get hurt. So, when I tell you to come, I am doing what I believe will keep you safe. Second, when you don't get what you want, you are not allowed to start screaming and crying. You are sinning against God and against me when you disobey and complain. I understand that you didn't want to leave the park. I know how difficult it is to show control when you don't get what you want. And because you can't control yourself, you need Jesus.
>
> Do you know what he did when he had to go somewhere he didn't want to go? He told God that he would do whatever God wanted him to do. He did that for you, and he did that for me. The place he didn't want to go was the cross. He knew the cross was going to be hard, and it would hurt him a lot.

But he did what he didn't want to do because he loved us. But I want you to know that you're not the only one getting disciplined today. Today God showed me his love by disciplining me, too. He showed me ways that I was being disobedient in my heart, too. He showed me my pride and my anger. Discipline hurts, but I have faith that God will use it in both of our lives to make us love him more.

Faith in God's Gracious Sovereignty

We want to free you from the unbelief and works righteousness that rob you of the comforts of grace. We want your parenting, though it seems difficult and never-ending, to be free from idolatry and unbelief. We want to encourage you to live by faith in the Son of God, who loves you and gave himself for you (Gal. 2:20), not by your own efforts.

Yes, we're to be faithful and diligent. But, even so, we are not guaranteed that our parenting will produce godly children. Let us say it again so that it begins to sink in: there are no promises in the Bible that even our best parenting will produce good children. None.

In fact, when you think about it, there are very few examples of godly parents producing godly children in the Bible. Think for a moment about the Old Testament saints who are known for serving the Lord. Abraham wasn't raised in a godly home. In fact, his father was an idolater. Joseph's dad sinfully favored him and disrespected his brothers because their mother wasn't as pretty as Joseph's. Moses was raised by an unmarried woman who worshiped the sun. David's dad thought so little of him that he didn't remember him when Samuel came looking for Israel's next king. Daniel's parents were idolaters and were judged by God in the exile.

On the other hand, we do have examples of children with terribly wicked parents who ended up serving the Lord faithfully. King Hezekiah is a good illustration of this. He was the son of one of the wickedest kings in Judah, Ahaz, but Hezekiah wasn't ruined by his father's wickedness. Instead, Hezekiah is famous for his faith and allegiance to the Lord. But Hezekiah had a son named Manasseh, who "led Judah and the inhabitants of Jerusalem astray, to do more evil than the nations whom the LORD destroyed before the people of Israel" (2 Chron. 33:9). Manasseh had a wicked son named Amon, but Amon had a righteous son named Josiah. There's a message for us here in this lineage: righteous fathers do not necessarily produce righteous children, and wicked fathers do not necessarily produce wicked children. In fact, it seems as though God delights in saving the children of his enemies. God delights in doing what we cannot do. He alone is Savior.

But what about Timothy? He had a believing mother and grandmother who had taught him the Scriptures (2 Tim. 1:5; 3:15). While it is true that Timothy had a good foundation from his mom and grandmother, he also had an unbelieving father who had refused to let him follow the faith of his mother (Acts 16:1–3). Timothy's dad wasn't an engaged, gospel-preaching, devotion-leading, righteous man. He wasn't even a believer, and he stopped Timothy's mother from giving the sign of the covenant to her child. *So God brought Paul to be a father to Timothy and to save him in spite of his father's unbelief.* Timothy fulfilled God's sovereign purpose by being a son to Paul, and Paul fulfilled God's purpose in being a father for Timothy. Moms who have unbelieving or disengaged husbands should rest in this truth and *never* fear that their husband's unbelief will close the doors of the kingdom to their children.

When we fall prey to the illusion that our good parenting will save our children's souls, we blindly forget that no one in the first churches were raised in gospel-centered homes. In fact, when you study the cultures in Corinth, Ephesus, or Rome, where infanticide was a normal practice and children were considered chattel, we should wonder that the early church was populated at all. No one in Jerusalem knew the secrets to successful parenting that would grant to their children the gift of faith in the Messiah, but the church was established anyway. That's because God can do all things, and no purpose of his can be thwarted (Job 42:2). He is the Savior.

There are no promises in the Bible of salvation, or even success, for faithful parenting. In fact, in the story that's normally called "the prodigal son" (Luke 15), Jesus described a good father who had two lost sons. One son was lost to immorality and the other to morality. Of course, in this story, the Father is God. If we say that good parents (as if there were such a thing!) always produce good kids, then God must not have been a good Father. You know that it's blasphemous even to think that way. Remember also that Jesus poured his life into twelve men for three years, and one of them betrayed him and fell utterly, and another denied him but was ultimately saved. Why were Judas and Peter such failures at Christ's hour of need? Was it because he hadn't taught them well enough, or did God's sovereign plan have something to do with it?

But What about Proverbs 22:6?

Okay, you might be thinking, *but what about Proverbs 22:6: "Train up a child in the way he should go; even when he is old he will not depart from it"?* Doesn't that verse teach that if we train our child in the right path, he will not depart from our training?

Understanding this verse begins with understanding the kind of literature the proverbs are. The proverbs are not conditional promises; they are maxims or wise sayings. They describe, in a general sense, the way that God has made the world run. But there are plenty of examples from which it's obvious that these maxims don't hold true all the time. Proverbs 10:4 is just one example: "A slack hand causes poverty, but the hand of the diligent makes rich." While it is generally true that hard work produces wealth, it's not always the case. There are plenty of hard-working rice farmers in India who will never even own a car and will wonder where their next meal is coming from. Another example is found in the proverb about the virtuous woman: "Her children rise up and call her blessed; her husband also, and he praises her" (Prov. 31:28). How many virtuous women have been scorned by children and husband only to be welcomed and honored by the Lord? Thousands? Millions?

The proverbs are not conditional promises; they are wise maxims. When we fail to understand this form of literature and build our lives on them as a guarantee, we end up with a philosophy akin to that of Job's comforters. They had a very simple formula for obtaining God's blessing: *Go and do the right thing.* Conversely, they believed that if someone lacks God's visible blessing, it must be because he is not doing what God wants him to do. They thought that faithful obedience always obligates God to respond in the way one desires. They were wrong (Job 42:7–8).

While it is true that God often graces wise parents with godly children, that is not always the case. God may use your parenting as means to draw your children to himself. But he may use other means and at a different time. Or he may use your child's rebellion and disinterest as a way to accomplish his unexpected will. Nothing we can do puts a lock on God's blessing us in the way we expect.

The Path of Faith

Why wouldn't God give us a sure promise that if we parent well, our children will do well? Wouldn't our parenting be more diligent if we thought we had the ability to save them? No, actually it wouldn't. We wouldn't work harder if we had that command and promise, because we don't respond well to commands. True obedience doesn't come from commands with promises. The nation of Israel and their response to Deuteronomy 28 and 29 ought to be enough proof of that.

God doesn't promise our children's salvation in response to our obedience, because he *never* encourages self-reliance. It would be against God's character to give us a promise that our children will be saved if we raise them in a certain way. That would mean that he was telling us to trust in something other than Christ and his grace and mercy. He would be encouraging us to trust in ourselves, and God never does that. The way of the Lord is always a way of faith—faith in his goodness, mercy, and love. Our faith is to be in him, not in ourselves.

Here's our hope: before time began God the Father saw us, each individually and distinctly. He not only saw us; he "knew" us. This means that he was intimately acquainted with everything about us before we even existed. He chose us in him to have relationship with him. He chose us as his children. But he didn't do this because of any good he saw in us. In fact, all of us have absolutely nothing to boast about. He chose us out of his sheer grace and because he loves loving the unlovely. Because of his great love he deserves to be fully honored by us. This means that we transfer our entire trust (and keep transferring it over and over again) to him. This is faith. In the same way that you trust in him and not in yourself for your salvation, you can trust in him for the salvation of your children. You can give yourself grace: he's in control, he is loving, his plan is best. And you can give your children grace, too. Parenting with grace isn't another set of rules for you to follow. It's a story that you're to rejoice in. Share the story with your children. Show them the Savior. Show them Jesus. Dazzle them with his love.

Here's Your Chore for the Day: Believe

At one point during Christ's earthly ministry, people came to him looking for a formula for successful living. They said to him, "What must we do, to be doing the works of God?" Jesus answered them, "This is the work of God, that you believe in him whom he has sent" (John 6:28–29).

They wanted the list. Can't you just hear their hearts? We can. *Just tell us what to do and we'll get about it. We know we can and we really want to, so just give us the list and we'll work it out.* Here was a great opportunity for the Lord to give them the law again. But he knew what they would do with it. He'd watched their response to it for thousands of years. He knew what was in their hearts (John 2:25). No, more rules was not what they needed. They needed faith. Do you want to do the work of God? Okay, then believe. Believe that God is strong enough to save your children, no matter how you fail. Believe that he is loving enough to bring them all the way into relationship with himself, whether you understand "grace parenting" or not. And believe that he is wise enough to know the right way and the right time to do it. What do you need to do? Simply believe: "Believe in the Lord Jesus, and you will be saved, you and your household" (Acts 16:31; see also Rom. 9:30–32; 10:3–4). In the words of Martin Luther with which we opened this chapter, "The law says, 'do this,' and it is never done. Grace says, 'believe in this,' and everything is already done." Everything is *already done*. Can you believe that? Will you?

Here's your invitation to take a ride in your parenting on what might initially feel like Mickey's Fun Wheel. All those rules about how to get your kids to "work the works of God" need to be left on the ground outside the gate. Step into the gondola and trust in him *alone*. Even though the tight buckles and restricting harnesses of the law might feel like a welcomed security to you, in the end they will chafe, and you'll want to throw them off. The law may serve for a time to keep your kids from rocking the cage too much, but eventually it will chafe against them, too. They will look for ways around it. The law cannot save them either. Tight buckles and restricting harnesses might make you *feel* more secure but the shocking truth is that you cannot control the direction of the gondola—you're completely at God's mercy. Does that frighten you? Why would it? Doesn't the gospel teach us that being at God's mercy is a place of rest and blessing? Isn't falling into his merciful arms a good thing?

We have no guarantees about the Lord's plan for our family, but one of the truths we are sure of is this: the law won't help. It won't help us orchestrate the future. It isn't powerful enough to change the hearts of our children. It won't enable us to obligate God to bless us because we won't keep it, and even if we work and work, it isn't the pathway to his blessing. He has told us what our work is to consist of: *belief*. Believing in the work Jesus Christ has already done. The Father wants us to rejoice in his beloved Son and rest in him alone.

Sure, giving them grace (instead of law) is scary. The law seems so reassuring, but it is a false assurance. It is only his grace that is sufficient to sustain and transform us. Grace is stronger than all our work and all our weakness and it is made perfect when we humble ourselves before God's desire to glorify his Son and not our great parenting (2 Cor. 12:9). Salvation is of the Lord—he is the Savior. Climb aboard and have a seat. No buckles here, just faith. Your loving Father has things well in hand. Believe.

Remembering God's Grace

Please don't ignore what the Holy Spirit might be doing in your heart through this chapter. Please do take the time to think deeply about it and answer the following questions.

1) In what ways have you believed the formula "*good parenting in, good children out*"? How is this formula contrary to the gospel?
2) Do you engage in works righteousness or idolatry when it comes to parenting? How?
3) If salvation is ultimately of the Lord, why does it matter how we discipline?
4) What are some ways you fail to believe in the goodness of God in your parenting?
5) How would resting completely in God change your relationship with your children?
6) Summarize in three or four sentences what you have learned in this chapter.

4

Jesus Loves All His Little Prodigals and Pharisees

One can be addicted to either lawlessness or lawfulness. Theologically there is no difference since both break relationship with God, the giver.
~ GERHARD O. FORDE[1]

Sparkling blue water and warm summer breezes; school's finally out and the kids are living in the pool. It is summer and all the neighborhood children are enjoying a fine game of Marco Polo with Susan and David.

While overseeing their fun, Mom is trying to grab a few rays of sunshine for herself. But then, with chagrin, she notices that the tone of the game has started to change. Groaning within herself, she thinks, *Here we go again! Why can't I have just one afternoon of rest without their fighting?*

"I quit!" David yells as he climbs out of the pool.

"You're such a cheater!" is Susan's angry rejoinder.

Those were just their beginning volleys. Feeling her own anger beginning to build, Mom quickly prays, *God, help me believe that this is you approaching me with grace. Please help me see and help me overcome my desire to be left alone. Please use this in our lives.*

Calling David and Susan to come to her, she welcomes them both into her arms. Both of them know what's coming, and their hard little faces reflect hearts determined not to listen.

David, younger than Susan by two years, regularly cheats at games to try to give himself an edge over his sister. David is the rule breaker who rationalizes that cheating is okay because he's littler and it's not fair that he has to lose all the time.

"David, I understand why you're tempted to cheat when you play games. I know that you want to win, but breaking rules, even the rules of a game like Marco Polo, is wrong. I know that it doesn't seem like a big deal to cheat at Marco Polo, but Jesus suffered and died for rule breakers."

"Yes, Mom," David replied. "I know and I'm sorry."

Although David is quick to say what he thinks are the magic words, his mom doubts that his "sorry" means anything more than, "Can we be done with this so I can get back in the pool?"

Next, Mom looks at her little rule keeper, Susan. She sees the hardness in Susan's eyes as she turns to her, asking her if screaming at her little brother was a kind thing to do.

Susan's response was a sullen no. But then the justification for her anger came rushing out. "But he always cheats! And then when we tell him to follow the rules, he always quits!"

Yes, Mom knew, that was true. David frequently cheated at games so that he could win. Susan rarely cheated, primarily because she usually won without much effort. Again Mom prayed for grace because she knew that Susan was right but also because she was tired of the continual conflict. *Lord,* she prayed, *help me be wise and know what to say now. Help me not to give into my own unbelief, works-righteousness, and idolatry. Help me see you here.*

"Susan," Mom began, "I agree with you. David should follow the rules. And I agree that we should remind him to do so." *What now? Something's missing here. Help me, Lord, please.* Then, once again, the gospel came rushing in on a tidal wave of grace.

"Yes, Susan, David should follow the rules of the game. But the rules are not the most important thing. There is something that is heavier and of more importance than the rules of Marco-Polo. Do you know what it is? Mercy is more important than the law."

This message confounded Susan, and a questioning look spread over her face. Even at the early age of nine, she had pretty much figured out that rules and law keeping were the be-all-to-end-all. She knew that rules were what makes you stay "right" and she loved feeling "right."

"Do you understand how mercy is more important than the law?"

Susan shook her head no. After all, what could be more important than keeping the rules and doing things right?

"Susan, let me tell you about something called the law of love."

"The law of love?" she asked. For the first time Susan's face and voice softened. Mom was beginning to have hope that the Holy Spirit would work in Susan's heart.

"Yes! The law of love is the law that Christ kept perfectly on your behalf. Let me tell you about it. We are all law-breaking rule-haters when it comes to something we want to do. David breaks the rules by cheating, you break the rules by screaming at him, and I break the rules by wanting peace and quiet. We're all law-breaking rule-haters. None of us keeps the rules or loves each other like we should. But when Jesus came, instead of making us pay for breaking the rules, he loved us. Do you know how he loved us?"

Susan knew the answer to this one, "By dying for our sin?"

"Yes, that is right! He took the punishment for our sin, to show us that something is more important than rules. Do you know what's more important? It is faith working though love, like Galatians 5:6 (MESSAGE) says: 'For in Christ, neither our most conscientious religion or disregard of religion amounts to anything. What matters is . . . faith expressed in love.' Our keeping the rules or not keeping the rules doesn't really count for anything before God. The only thing that counts is belief that Jesus died for us and after that responding in love for God and each other.

"So you see, Susan, if you truly believe that Jesus died for your sin, you can love your rule-breaking little brother. After all, you are just like him. And when you fail to love him, you can remember that Jesus, the Lord of love, has obeyed the rule about love for you in your place, so that, if you truly believe it, your desire to feel like a 'good' person has been forever satisfied in the goodness of God's Son. And then, because of how beautiful he is and how beautiful his love for you is, you can get back in the water and play, remembering that loving your brother the way Christ loved you is more important than following the rules of Marco Polo."

Mom looked with love and understanding at both her children. Their faces were softer; they were beginning to comprehend the good news. "Now, let me pray that the Holy Spirit helps you both to understand what we just talked about. Then, if you are truly sorry for your anger toward each other, you can ask each other and the Lord for forgiveness. After we pray, I'll leave the two of you to talk for a few minutes before you get back into the pool."

Within every household and even within the heart of every person, there is a Susan and a David. There are those who love thinking that they keep the rules, and there are those who don't care about the rules as much as they care about other things, such as winning or having a good time. The heart of a Susan and a David resides within each of us, and who shows up simply depends on what's at stake on any given day. Do we want to win? Do we want to rest? Do we want to claim the moral high ground? Welcome, Susan and David. The only power strong enough to transform the selfishly rebellious and the selfishly self-righteous heart is grace. The law doesn't transform the heart of either Susan or David. It only hardens them in pride and despair.

The Story of the Welcoming Father

Most of us are familiar with the story Jesus told that is recorded in Luke 15:11–32:

> There was a man who had two sons. And the younger of them said to his father, "Father, give me the share of property that is coming to me." And he divided his property between them. Not many days later, the younger son gathered all he had and took a journey into a far country, and there he squandered his property in reckless living. And when he had spent everything, a severe famine arose in that country, and he began to be in need. So he went and hired himself out to one of the citizens of that country, who sent him into his fields to feed pigs. And he was longing to be fed with the pods that the pigs ate, and no one gave him anything.
>
> But when he came to himself, he said, "How many of my father's hired servants have more than enough bread, but I perish here with hunger! I will arise and go to my father, and I will say to him, 'Father, I have sinned against heaven and before you. I am no longer worthy to be called your son. Treat me as one of your hired servants.'" And he arose and came to his father. But while he was still a long way off, his father saw him and felt compassion, and ran and embraced him and kissed him. And the son said to him, "Father, I have sinned against heaven and before you. I am no longer worthy to be called your son." But the father said to his servants, "Bring quickly the best robe, and put it on him, and put a ring on his hand, and shoes on his feet. And bring the fattened

calf and kill it, and let us eat and celebrate. For this my son was dead, and is alive again; he was lost, and is found." And they began to celebrate.

Now his older son was in the field, and as he came and drew near to the house, he heard music and dancing. And he called one of the servants and asked what these things meant. And he said to him, "Your brother has come, and your father has killed the fattened calf, because he has received him back safe and sound." But he was angry and refused to go in. His father came out and entreated him, but he answered his father, "Look, these many years I have served you, and I never disobeyed your command, yet you never gave me a young goat, that I might celebrate with my friends. But when this son of yours came, who has devoured your property with prostitutes, you killed the fattened calf for him!" And he said to him, "Son, you are always with me, and all that is mine is yours. It was fitting to celebrate and be glad, for this your brother was dead, and is alive; he was lost, and is found."

Although this parable is usually known as "the prodigal son," a better name for it might be something like "the welcoming father." Why "welcoming father"? Because the astounding lesson of this parable is that an utterly good father welcomes two wicked sons who were outwardly very different but inwardly exactly the same.

One of the sons was like our little David: tired of being youngest, anxious to prove his manhood, cavalier about the rules. He set out with his inheritance to free himself from the shadow of his brother's crushing goodness. And he accomplished his goal. He slid from an elevated place of status and position in the community down and down into a pig trough. He had thoroughly degraded himself; he was desolate, starving, and desperate for rescue. Children like David will break your heart.

The other son was like our Susan. He loved feeling right and prided himself on keeping the rules. And now that his brother had left, he really relished the fact that he had won the battle of "best son," too. He felt that he had finally and fully secured all his father's blessing.

If your parenting is moralistic, like most of ours is, children like David will break your heart, but children like Susan will make you proud. It is only when you parent with grace that the destitution of both children becomes apparent. Children who embarrass you and children who make you proud must both be taught the deeper truth of the welcoming father: mercy trumps law.

So, although the two sons are integral to the story, they aren't the main characters. No, the main character in this story is the father who joyfully welcomes both Susan and David to his table. Hear the father's heart in Christ's description of his welcome of the younger son, "But while he was still a long way off, his father saw him and felt compassion, and ran and embraced him and kissed him" (Luke 15:20). The father warmly embraces his smelly, destitute, gaunt son, and the first thing he does is reestablish his place in the family. He gives him the ring, the robe, the feast.

The Susans of the world are not hoping for their errant brother's return. No, of course not. They're out working. And they are filled with proud resentment at the father's welcome home party for his son. But what is the father's response to such arrogance? "His father came out and entreated him" (Luke 15:28). The father's arms are open wide: "Son, you are always with me, and all that is mine is yours" (v. 31).

The father's loving welcome extends to both sons although neither one is worthy or deserving in any way. The father has a higher rule, a greater law: merciful love. Our children, both the "bad" ones and the "good" ones, need to hear his message of entreaty: "My arms are open to you; all that is mine is yours. Come and delight in my generous mercy."

Begrudge God's Generosity—Who Would Do That?

At the end of another parable, after describing disgruntled laborers in a vineyard (Matt. 20:1–16), Jesus poses two penetrating questions: "Am I not allowed to do what I choose with what belongs to me? Or do you begrudge my generosity?" (v. 15) None of us would ever say that we resent God's generous mercy, would we? When we stop and consider our salvation, we're filled with gratitude for his generosity. We know that we've been saved by grace alone through faith alone.

But has that gratitude for grace made it all the way down into the way we raise our children? Could it be that in our parenting we pretend that God plays by our rules? Do we believe that he is obligated to bestow his gifts in a way that coincides with our sense of right and wrong? Here's how this mistake may play out in our foundational beliefs: we're very comfortable thinking, "Good parenting in, good children out," aren't we? And we teach our children this maxim: "Good behavior in, God's smile out."

This is the mistake the disgruntled laborers in this parable made. They thought there should be a one-for-one correlation between their work and the master's reward. Then, when the master refused to acquiesce to their expectations, they became envious and angry. The problem, of course, is that God is not a cosmic vending machine (assuming we've got enough quarters to make any difference to him). And, thankfully, law is not all there is, either. There is something more, something that overrules law—there is God's happiness and delight in his generous mercy. There is grace.

The Gospel Is for Sinners

So, how can we teach our children to rejoice in God's generous mercy and love? We know that we need to train them in rules for obedience; that's obvious. But how can we teach them about something so outside the norm, such as God's joy in being merciful to sinners?

The first way we do that is to see and confess our propensity to live like one of the two sons. Confess to your David that you, too, break the rules and that you always justify yourself for doing so. Alternately, confess to Susan that you, too, love to rely on the rules and to feel superior to others.

Being specific about the ways you are simultaneously proud and disobedient will help your children understand that *the gospel is for sinners.* The gospel is not good news to those who pride themselves on their hard work. It is infuriating news. But it is good news to younger-brother types who are tempted to turn away from the faith fairly early on because they don't think that the gospel is for sinners. They think it is for good people who like being "gooder."

Consistent, transparent, and specific confession of sin will help children see how their parents struggle with sin in the same ways that they do. This dynamic is especially important if there is a highly successful elder-brother type in the home. Teaching David that he and Susan and Mom and Dad are all lost, all sick, all in need of salvation is so very crucial, whereas saying things like, "Why can't you be more like Susan?" obliterates the gospel message. It tells David that there is something intrinsically wrong with him that isn't wrong with Susan. It destroys his hope of ever hearing God's benediction of goodness over his life. It breeds unbelief and despair. And, it is false.

God finds great joy in welcoming dirty, starving Davids to his table. And because they feel their lostness so keenly, they may more easily recognize their need for the Rescuer. Their lives are usually messier and more dramatic, but they're also more authentic and can be greatly used by the Lord because they know they've been forgiven for so much.

As much as David needs to hear about your struggle with sin, Susan needs it even more. She's usually the parent pleaser who honestly enjoys making you happy and thinks that your happiness and God's are analogous. What she desperately needs is to realize that her parents are deeply sinful, even though the gospel has made them love holiness. Specific confession of pride, judging, criticism, envy, and selfish ambition will help Susan understand her own propensities to fail in the same ways, while praising Susan for being a "good girl" will breed toxic pride in her heart. It will teach her that she isn't all that bad. She won't recognize her need for the Rescuer, although she may say that she's a Christian. What does Susan need to hear? She needs to hear that her desire to prove her own worthiness is one of the greatest hindrances to faith that she'll ever face.

Of course, our confession of sin is to be moderated by wisdom. We never want to confess to our children that we don't really like them very much or that we wish that they had never been born. This kind of information will not bless them with freedom to admit their own sinfulness or to trust us.

In addition, we should be careful about the categories of sin that we confess. There are certain sins that children can't understand or that are private matters between the adults in the family. A good rule for confession is that it is appropriate to confess any sin that the children have become aware of or any sin that has affected them personally. If you've been sinfully angry because your time by the pool has been interrupted, you can fully disclose your heart to your children and ask them for forgiveness and for prayer. When they overhear you speaking in a proud, unkind way about someone, you can confess that too.

Most parents know enough to confess their anger to their children. But do we regularly confess our self-righteousness and pride? Saying something like, "I can't believe you would do something like that!" or a slight coldness followed by a disapproving look, should be followed by, "Please forgive me for forgetting that you and I are just the same. We both sin. When I say things like that, I am being self-righteous and forgetting that Jesus had to die for my sins too. I'm sure that my words were demeaning, but that's not all they were. They were also against the truth of the gospel. Please forgive me and pray for me that the Lord will help me remember all the ways that I sin too and that he'll make me humble and thankful for grace."

Calling All Sinners

In the following narrative we see both Susan and David. How does the Savior comfort and confront each one?

> As Jesus reclined at table in the house, behold, many tax collectors and sinners came and were reclining with Jesus and his disciples. And when the Pharisees saw this, they said to his disciples, "Why does your teacher eat with tax collectors and sinners?" But when he heard it, he said, "Those who are well have no need of a physician, but those who are sick. Go and learn what this means, 'I desire mercy, and not sacrifice.' For I came not to call the righteous, but sinners." (Matt. 9:10–13)

Echoing the prophet Hosea, Jesus flipped everything in our quid pro quo world on its head. Instead of commending those who were outwardly good, he demeaned them and sent them back to school. Although they prided themselves on being good and obeying the law, they had completely misread God's nature and purpose. This ignorance calcified their hearts, denuding love for God and blinding them to the needs of their neighbor. They did not see their need of rescue and missed the day of their visitation (Luke 19:44). Only sinners who know that they are sinners will hear the word "mercy" spoken over them. Susan and David need to know that they are sinners—that the gospel is for sinners—and that there is a rescuer who loves pouring out mercy on those who cannot help themselves.

Give grace to your children today by speaking of sin and mercy. Tell Susan that she can relax into God's loving embrace and stop thinking that she has to perform in order to get her welcoming Father to love her. Tell David that he can have hope that even though he really struggles, he's the very sort of person Jesus loved being around. Dazzle them with his love.

It's obvious to us how easy it is for parents to be both lazy prodigals and demanding Pharisees—on the same day! We are lazy and apathetic when we'd rather sit by the pool and just give the kids a time-out when they fight or, better yet, just ignore them and hope that they work it out on their own. Who wants to take time to talk about anything? They never listen anyway. When is it our day to rest? On the other hand, we are demanding rule keepers when we take God's law and incessantly whack them over the head with it: "God says you must be honest and never cheat. I can't believe you would sin like that! Don't you know that cheating is like lying, and liars go to hell?" Or, "Susan, you're always so unkind. I think you need to memorize that passage from Ephesians 4 about kindness again. Go do it and then come and tell me when you're truly sorry. Now, go apologize to your brother."

What's truly amazing is that Jesus Christ loves both rule breakers and rule keepers. And because of his Son's perfect obedience, both of them can be called "beloved sons." When the believing rule breaker sins he can look up and say, "Jesus is my righteousness." And when the believing rule keeper realizes her self-righteousness, she too can look up and say, "Jesus is my righteousness."

Do Not Hinder Them

We sit together on the bench swing, cozying up under our lap blankets, and we sing. We sing many songs but the one that we love best is this:

> Jesus loves me, this I know,
> For the Bible tells me so.
> Little ones to him belong,
> They are weak, but he is strong.[2]

What a comfort it is to rest in the knowledge that although we are weak, his love is strong enough to welcome us right up onto his lap. Here is the precious passage where we get a glimpse of this sweet love:

> They were bringing children to him that he might touch them, and the disciples rebuked them. But when Jesus saw it, he was indignant and said to them, "Let the children come to me; do not hinder them, for to such belongs the kingdom of God. Truly, I say to you, whoever does not receive the kingdom of God like a child shall not enter it." And he took them in his arms and blessed them, laying his hands on them. (Mark 10:13–16)

Can't you just imagine this scene? Here are the disciples, filled with ambition and self-righteousness. *Children? Women bringing children? Oh, no. Children are, well, children, and they aren't really important in the grand scheme of things. They haven't learned all that we know about how to get in good with God. Climb up on his lap? Never!*

The disciples had failed their kingdom entrance exam. Like the religious leaders, like the elder brother, like Susan, like most of us, they assumed that being important, grown up, responsible, and good were the ways to get close to God. They were wrong. Can't you see their shock and wonder when he opened his arms and pulled the little ones up onto his lap? He listened to their stories. He drew them close. He smiled warmly. He laughed at their jokes. They had nothing to offer, nothing to give to him. All they had was responsive, humble, messy love. They loved him because he had loved them. And his love was all they needed.

Jesus was indignant with his disciples because they tried to hinder the children from coming to him. How could we hinder children from coming to the Lord? We get a clue when we look at the context of this story sandwiched as it is between two others. The first one is about the Pharisee and the tax collector who both went up to pray. Luke tells us that the point of the parable is that some people trusted that they were righteous (treating others with contempt) and others brought only a plea for mercy, a plea that was quickly answered.

> But the tax collector, standing far off, would not even lift up his eyes to heaven, but beat his breast, saying, "God, be merciful to me, a sinner!" I tell you, this man went down to his house justified, rather than the other. For everyone who exalts himself will be humbled, but the one who humbles himself will be exalted. (Luke 18:13–14)

We hinder our children from enjoying God's embrace when we teach them that their religious activity and obedience elevates them out of the category of sinner in need of mercy. This was the attitude of both the disciples and the religious leaders. Women, children, sinners, Gentiles, the disabled, and the poor were all marginalized and insignificant. But it was just those sorts of people the Lord loved to draw into his embrace. We hinder our children from coming to him when we inadvertently teach them that the good news is meant for good people.

The story that follows Jesus's encounter with moms and kids is about a rich, young ruler who had done everything his father had told him. He was a good boy who had grown into a good man. He was the quintessential elder brother who wanted to add Jesus's good teaching to his portfolio. He thought he could work the works of God. Even so, he had some sort of niggling sense that he wasn't quite right, because he was looking for advice on eternal life. Keepers of the law *never* have full assurance, because they know their own heart. Deep down, hidden away in a locked closet of the rich, young ruler's heart, was the truth that he had never perfectly obeyed. Would he be able to see past his self-righteousness into mercy?

We read his story in Luke 18:18–27. Approaching Jesus with the blessed benediction the young man asked him, "Good Teacher, what must I do to inherit eternal life?" Dismissing the contradiction between wages and an inheritance, Jesus posed a deeper question: "Why do you call me good? No one is good except God alone." Jesus begins confronting the man's self-trust by questioning him: *Are you saying that I am God? Do you know that you aren't good?* The Lord then recited five of the ten commandments, to which this young man replied: "All these I have kept from my youth" (v. 21). Imagine that. This young man really did think he was good. He had never taken something that belonged to someone else—wife, life, or goods; he had never lied, and he had always honored his parents. What a résumé! Of course, Jesus purposely skipped the laws about worship, false gods, and coveting, preferring instead to allow this young ruler time to think. Then Jesus swung God's hammer and the death blow was dealt: "One thing you still lack. Sell all that you have and distribute to the poor, and you will have treasure in heaven; and come, follow me" (v. 22).

In less than one minute, Jesus annihilated decades of punctilious law keeping. *There's only one small problem, you see. You don't love your neighbor and you don't love God. You love your goodness and your riches. You think you're good, but you're actually bankrupt and sinful.* Jesus knowingly commanded him to do something he was unwilling and unable to do. This man could no more renounce what he loved than a camel can go through the eye of a needle—and he knew it. Jesus meant to crush him. What was the response of our dear young man? "He became very sad, for he was extremely rich" (v. 23).

The response of the people listening in on this incident was utter amazement. *Wow! If this good fellow who has everything going for him and is so religious can't be saved, who can?* In other words, if rich, good people can't make it in, what hope do we have? Who can make it in? Only people who have been made to know that they need mercy. Jesus answers, "What is impossible with men is possible with God" (v. 27).

With God Nothing Is Impossible

We can imagine that some of you may be feeling like you've done everything wrong. You may see your errors or be uncomfortably aware that you've missed the message of grace. So, here's a sip of gospel grace for you: as parents, our only hope for our children's salvation lies in the rich mercy of a compassionate God and the atoning work of our perfect representative, Jesus Christ. Then, when we consistently and unashamedly throw ourselves on God's mercy, we will help our children place their hope in him too.

We will teach them that this is a hope that "we who have fled for refuge might have strong encouragement to hold fast to" (Heb. 6:18). This hope is a "sure and steadfast anchor of the soul, a hope that enters into the inner place behind the curtain, where Jesus has gone as a forerunner on our behalf, having become a high priest forever" (vv. 19–20). It is a hope that is built on nothing less than Jesus's blood and righteousness:

> My hope is built on nothing less
> than Jesus' blood and righteousness.
> I dare not trust the sweetest frame,
> but wholly lean on Jesus' name.[3]

We dare not trust our sweetest efforts or their sweetest responses. Instead, we wholly lean on Jesus's name. He is loving. He is good. He is powerful. He's done it all.

As we close this chapter we want to leave you with a comforting message that must never be forgotten: *the disciples couldn't hinder the children from coming to him even though they tried.* When God calls our children to come to him, even if we haven't gotten it all right, even if we've trained little Pharisees or have a house full of prodigals, nothing is impossible for him. He can break through all our flawed methods and redeem all our frail errors. The world tells us that our children's success depends upon our success. The world knows nothing of God's ability to use our failures as means to bless. "What is impossible with men is possible with God" (Luke 18:27).

So, even though we desire to be the ones who place our children in the lap of God's mercy and even though we stumble so badly trying to do so, Jesus is strong enough to pick each of us up and carry us all the way. Parents, too, are weak but Jesus is strong. No one, not even you, can thwart his purpose to bless those who are his (Eph. 1:11).

Remembering God's Grace

Please don't ignore what the Holy Spirit might be doing in your heart through this chapter. Do take the time to think deeply about it and answer the questions.

1) Have you ignored your little Pharisees' need for a Savior? How can you help the Pharisees in your house see the greater law?
2) Is teaching your children about God's generous love and mercy a new way of parenting for you? How? Have you been more concerned with teaching them about obedience?
3) How can we teach our children that the gospel is for sinners?
4) Have you hindered your children from coming to Jesus? In what ways?
5) When looking at our parenting, where does our only comfort come from?
6) Summarize in three or four sentences what you have learned in this chapter.

part two

Evidences of Grace

5

Grace That Trains

Grace does not forbid giving directions, promises, corrections, and warnings. Only cruelty would forbid such help.
~ **BRYAN CHAPELL**[1]

Over the previous four chapters we have bombarded you with one message: give your children grace. We've encouraged you to dazzle them with the message of Christ's love and welcome, and then when you think that surely they must be tiring of it, go back and drench them with it again. Steep their little parched souls in the blessings of the good news: *Jesus Christ has already done all the work that needed to be done.* When in great relief from excruciating agony of soul he declared, "It is finished," it really was. This is the message that we and our children need to hear over and over again.

We have reminded you of this because every human heart is always and ever drawn to law. In the same way that iron filings follow a magnet, our hearts chase after rules—not because we ever really obey them but because we think they make life manageable. Rules elevate us to the position of lawgiver; they help us avoid the humiliation of prostrating ourselves before a bloody, despicable cross. We love to try to approve of ourselves and control others by generating more and more rules. "Our desire to please God, combined with the human bent to prove our acceptance by comparison with and control of others, makes us factories of human legislation."[2]

"Factories of human legislation"—yes, that is surely what we are. We love multiplied rules and charts and posted placards. We trust in them to help us make life tidy, controllable, crisp. Got a problem? Make a rule! But by disparaging rules, are we saying that all rules are to be avoided? Does grace negate the necessity for law? Should we simply ignore our children's behavior and only speak of God's love? Is that what real grace looks like?

Grace That Disciplines

"Grace does not forbid giving directions, promises, corrections, and warnings. Only cruelty would forbid such help."[3] Parents are to discipline, instruct, train, and nurture their children. Only a cold detachment or a selfish disdain for children's desperate need for direction would cause us to refuse to train them. It would be a catastrophic failure to love if we left them on their own. In fact, it would be a complete negation of familial relationship and responsibility.

> If you are left without discipline, in which all have participated, then you are illegitimate children and not sons. (Heb. 12:8)

Discipline proves relationship. Instruction demonstrates love. Grace is not averse to training. In fact, one of the functions of grace *is* training in righteousness:

> For the grace of God has appeared, bringing salvation for all people, *training us* to renounce ungodliness and worldly passions, and to live self-controlled, upright, and godly lives in the present age, waiting for our blessed hope, the appearing of the glory of our great God and Savior Jesus Christ, who gave himself for us to redeem us from all lawlessness and to purify for himself a people for his own possession who are zealous for good works. (Titus 2:11–14)

In the preceding passage, Paul shows us how grace trains us. First, it trains us by reminding us of all that God has already done for us in Christ: he's appeared to us; he has brought us salvation; he has redeemed, purified, and purchased us, and promised to return for us; and he is changing us so that we will be zealous for good works. It is into this context of gospel declarations that training in discipline, or gospel obligation, is given: because of his great love, we are to renounce ungodliness and worldly passions and live self-controlled, upright, and godly lives. Paul never tires of reminding us of the declarations of the gospel. But he also never ignores our obligatory response. The Holy Spirit teaches us of the glories of Jesus, *and* he trains us to be holy. Grace trains us to rest in what Christ has done for us *and* to live lives of godly gratitude.

All parents, whether they've tasted grace or not, have been given the great privilege and responsibility of being their children's principal teachers. During the first few hours of life, a mother teaches her baby to trust her to provide his physical needs. She teaches him how to nurse, she swaddles him so that he feels warm, secure, loved. As he grows, godly parents will continue to provide for him and swaddle him in loving discipline as they help him taste and see that the Lord is good (Ps. 34:8). It is God's kindness to mankind that he gives children parents. It is his grace that teaches us how to train them.

The Nurture and Admonition of the Lord

In light of the number of books that have been written about parenting, the following statement may seem somewhat shocking: *there are only two passages in the New Testament that give direct commands concerning it*. Both are terse and to the point and are given without any profound explanation. They both contain a warning to fathers (and by implication to mothers who train children alongside them). The first is Ephesians 6:4: "Fathers, do not provoke your children to anger, but bring them up in the discipline and instruction of the Lord." The second is Colossians 3:21: "Fathers, do not provoke your children, lest they become discouraged."

Even though these two commands seem very basic and straightforward, perhaps we've failed to apprehend their true meaning. Perhaps the key to understanding discipline and instruction that is markedly Christian is assumed in the simple phrase that most of us failed to take into account when we read the preceding verses: "of the Lord." Here is the Ephesians passage again, "Fathers, do not provoke your children to anger, but bring them up in the discipline and instruction *of the Lord*."[4]

Generally speaking, whenever Paul uses the phrase "of the Lord," he is referring specifically to the Lord Jesus Christ.[5] Now, stop and think with us for a moment. Would the uniqueness of Christian parenting be clearer to you if this passage read, "Fathers, do not provoke your children to anger, but bring them up in the discipline and instruction of Jesus Christ"? Would that rewording spur you to think more specifically about him, about his work? What would the discipline and instruction of Jesus look like? By suggesting this change in wording, we are not suggesting that we know better than the Holy Spirit how to craft Scripture. It's simply that the phrase "of the Lord" has become hackneyed "Christianeze" to many of us. We hardly see it when we read it. It doesn't carry the same weight with us that it carried with them. It was fresh and astounding and paradigm-shattering when they heard it. *Of the Lord?* they would wonder, *What does that mean?* The Jews knew what the discipline and instruction of the rabbis looked like. The Greeks understood the discipline and instruction of the philosophers. But the discipline and instruction *of the Lord? Of Jesus?* What was that?

To help you get a better handle on what this "of the Lord" parenting entails, let's imagine for a moment that Paul had penned this phrase instead: Parents, "bring up your children in the discipline and instruction of the law." How would those three words, "of the law," change the focus and method of your parenting? Or would they?

On the other hand, in the ancient Near East, Gentile (Ephesian, Colossian) children were trained in the discipline and instruction "of Greek philosophers." They were instructed in logic and rhetoric and taught how to define and live a good life based on the teachings of men like Aristotle, Socrates, and Plato. The novel, radical message of grace turned everything they believed about parenting upside down. They wondered the same thing you do. "'Of the Lord'—what does that mean?"

Neither the Jews nor the Greeks would naturally have employed training that was "of the Lord." This phrase would have been peculiar to them. Paul meant it to be so. Those steeped in the law and those steeped in worldly philosophies would have had to think deeply about the implications of the good news as they sought to faithfully parent their children—just like we do. Here are a few clarifying questions that might help you get a better handle on what "of the Lord" parenting looks like:

- *How does the incarnation change the way you speak to your children?* God became a child. That one act of condescension and identification should forever stop us from denigrating children. The incarnation would have astonished them. To them, children were chattel, property to be disposed of at a father's whim.

- *What about the resurrection?* Does the truth of Christ's victory over sin and death make any difference when our kids struggle with ongoing sin? How? In the resurrection Jesus brought justification to those who believe, including our believing children (Rom. 4:24–25). If they are justified, God looks at them not only as those who have never sinned but as those who have always obeyed. How would this truth change your parenting?

- *Have you ever helped them understand what his ascension and ongoing reign means when their best friend moves out of town?* What does the eternal priesthood of the God-Man mean when they suffer loss? That he "always lives to make intercession for them" (Heb. 7:25) and suffered in every way can bring deep comfort to a child who feels that he is alone and friendless.

Learning to apply the truths of the incarnation, sinless life, substitutionary death, bodily resurrection, ascension, reign, and return of the Lord Jesus Christ is what it means to raise your children in the nurture and admonition "of the Lord." Sadly, very few of us have ever even begun to do this. Instead, like parents before us we train children in the tradition of our favorite rabbis and pop psychology. We need to learn what "of the Lord" parenting means.

In Ephesians, Paul employs two different words: *discipline* and *instruction*. The word for discipline, *paideia*, means to "nurture, educate, or *train*," and the word for instruction, *nouthesia*, means "calling attention to" or "mild rebuke," "*correction*," or "warning." In other words, Paul is saying that the way Christian parents are to bring children up is by nurturing, correcting, and training them *in the truth of or about Jesus Christ*. Paul is telling parents to daily proclaim the message about Jesus to their children and to warn or rebuke them when they forget to live in the light of what Jesus had already done. He was telling them to tether every aspect of their parenting to the gospel message.

Manage, Nurture, and Love

Because the Bible is not primarily a manual on childrearing but a proclamation of the good news, and because the passages in the New Testament that directly address it are very few in number (actually just the two we've looked at), we're going to look at four other passages that describe what "of the Lord" parenting would look like, without giving actual direction on how to do it.

The first two of these passages describe faithful parenting as one of the qualifications for male leaders. In 1 Timothy 3:4–6,[6] a man is qualified to be considered for eldership if he has "managed" his children, keeping them in submission. Likewise in 1 Timothy 3:12–13, a deacon is to have "managed" his household and children well.[7] Both elders and deacons (and their wives) are called to oversee or manage the spiritual and natural affairs of the church. The home is the primary training ground for a man's growth in management skills. There, in the home with his own flesh and blood, a father also learns how to appeal to those under his oversight to respond submissively to the Lord's authority through him.

Christian parents are to *manage* or oversee and admonish their children.[8] Christian children are to submit to the management and direction of their parents. How do we help our children develop such submissiveness? A submissive heart is always the fruit of humility, an understanding of our helplessness and frailty. The humility that acquiesces to being led, managed, and trained flows out of an understanding of one's own lostness and a growing understanding of and trust in God's great offer of life. Only the good news of the gospel produces a truly submissive humility of heart.

The third and fourth descriptive passages focus more specifically on a mother's role. The first of these two gives the qualifications of a widow deserving of assistance from the church. A widow should be considered worthy of the church's support if she has "brought up children" (1 Tim. 5:10). This Greek phrase, also translated "nourished" or "nurtured," describes one of the primary roles of a mother. Moms feed and nourish their children, both physically and spiritually. Women are *nurturers*. It is in both our physical design, as those who nourish babies from our own body, and in our personality, as those who seek to meet the needs of those in our care whenever we can. Paul pictured his ministry among the Thessalonians in this same way:

> But we were gentle among you, like a nursing mother taking care of her own children. So, being affectionately desirous of you, we were ready to share with you not only the gospel of God but also our own selves, because you had become very dear to us. (1 Thess. 2:7–8; see also Isa. 66:13)

We find the fourth passage in Titus 2:4, where we learn that older women are to "train" younger women to love their children. One might wonder why mothers would need to be trained to love their children until we recollect our own natural propensity to selfishness and laziness. Younger women are to be encouraged to be fond of and affectionate with their children, rather than pouring out all their affection on themselves or their girlfriends.

In summary then, the New Testament indirectly teaches fathers and mothers to manage or oversee their children; to teach them humility and submission; to nurture them physically, spiritually, and emotionally; and to love them dearly.

Words from the Old Testament

Right about now you might be wondering about all those passages in the Old Testament that speak of parenting. Let's take a few moments to peruse them, too, as we seek to construct a methodology for parenting that is both biblical and "of the Lord."

Genesis 18:19 is the first passage in the Bible that describes a father's responsibilities. God states that his relationship with his son Abraham began by God's choice, not Abraham's: "For I have chosen him." Then, in response to God's gracious choice, Abraham is to "command his children and his household after him to keep the way of the LORD by doing righteousness and justice." Because of God's initiating grace in his life, Abraham was to command or train his children to keep the way of the Lord.

On other occasions the Lord sketches likely dialog between parents and their children. The Lord assumes that upon a child's seeing his parents observe a feast day or recite the law, the child will ask, "What does this mean?" Notice carefully that in every case the answer to the question of meaning is never primarily our obligation but rather *promises of* God's grace. Here are some examples of proper answers and other instructions that ought to be implemented in day-to-day conversation:

- "And when your children say to you, 'What do you mean by this service?' you shall say, 'It is the sacrifice of the LORD's Passover, for he passed over the houses of the people of Israel in Egypt, when he struck the Egyptians but spared our houses'" (Ex. 12:26–27).

- "And when in time to come your son asks you, 'What does this mean?' you shall say to him, 'By a strong hand the LORD brought us out of Egypt, from the house of slavery'" (Ex. 13:14; see also vv. 15–16; Deut. 6:20–7:1; Josh. 4:21–23).

- "Only take care, and keep your soul diligently, lest you forget the things that your eyes have seen, and lest they depart from your heart all the days of your life. Make them known to your children and your children's children" (Deut. 4:9; see also vv. 10–14).

- Because the Lord has loved us and made such great promises to us, we are to teach our children to love him with all their heart, all their soul, and all their might. When should we teach this to them? All the time: "You . . . shall talk of them when you sit in your house, and when you walk by the way, and when you lie down, and when you rise" (Deut. 6:7–8; see also 11:19–21).

- The psalmist longed to proclaim to "another generation, your power to all those to come. Your righteousness, O God, reaches the high heavens. You who have done great things, O God, who is like you?" (Ps. 71:18–19).

- "We will not hide them from their children, but tell to the coming generation the glorious deeds of the LORD, and his might, and the wonders that he has done" (Ps. 78:4).

What should be obvious by now is that even Old Testament parents didn't discipline and instruct their children solely in the law. They, too, were to give them the promises of grace because they had been given grace, and only grace changes the heart. The law was always given *subsequent* to God's initiating mercy and always in the context of relationship with his children, *never* as a way to earn his blessing.

(We know that you may be wondering about the role of the book of Proverbs in parenting that is "of the Lord." You may also be wondering about the use of physical correction that Proverbs enjoins. Because this is such an important topic, we've devoted an entire chapter to it, coming up right after this one.)

Now, in light of what we've learned about parenting so far, here are five different categories we've talked about: manage, nurture, train, correct, and promise. To help you see how to practically apply these truths to your everyday life, here's how they might shape your "of the Lord" parenting when your son or daughter is unhappy after making the last out in a baseball game.

Here are the five categories from chart 5.1: **Management, Nurturing, Training, Correction**, and rehearsing gospel **Promises**. (In Appendix 2 we've furnished you with more examples using this chart in different situations.)

Management

Is this a time to simply manage your children? Sometimes children just need to be told what to do: "Go get in the car now." "Don't run in the street!" "Finish your homework and get ready for bed." "Sit quietly in church." "Don't throw your bat." Management includes training in the social, civic, and religious categories we talked about in chapter 1. A chart outlining everyone's daily responsibilities can help you manage the home, but, again, care should be taken not to confuse compliance to management rules with true Christian righteousness. Management charts may help you run the home more smoothly. They may also become your god. Management is simply your effort to control outward behavior. It is not meant to get to the heart, although a child's obedience to the outward rules *may* be evidences of faith. Every parent has to manage her child's behavior.

Nurturing

Many times children simply need hope that there is a God who loves them and has provided everything they need. Feed their soul with gospel truths of how Jesus has cared for them. One mom, whose daughter was being rebellious, laid out breakfast for her every morning with a little something special, like a flower or some blueberries. Her daughter later told her that the Lord had used these little tokens to melt her heart. Even if your child refuses to open up to you or listen to you, you can still nurture her heart.

Training

Children also need to learn how the gospel applies to the circumstance they're facing and what an appropriate response should be. For instance, you could say something like this:

> Yes, losing is difficult, especially when the team's loss is your fault. Jesus Christ understands losing because he lost relationship with his Father on the cross. He understands shame and humiliation because he was stripped

and mocked and called a blasphemer. All this he willingly suffered for his children. This means that losing a baseball game is not the worst thing that could ever happen. Losing Jesus Christ is, and he's promised never to leave us or forsake us. Your sinful response to your loss should make you thankful that he paid the price for your sin and loves you still.

Chart 5.1: "Of the Lord" Parenting

Category	Scripture	Example
Management or Oversight	I Tim. 3:4–6; 12–13; Gal. 4:2–3	**Basic Instructions for daily living:** "Throwing your bat when you strike out is inappropriate behavior. You could hurt someone."
Gospel **Nurturing:** "Bring them up"	Ps. 78:4; 17–19; I Thess. 2:6–8; I Tim. 5:10	**Feeding their souls with grace:** "I know you're sad because your team lost. I'm sad too. Let's look up now at how high the heavens are above the earth. This is how much God loves you. He's using this suffering in your life to make us both look up and see his love" (Ps. 103:11–12)
Gospel **Training:** "Of the Lord"	Eph. 6:4; Col. 3:24	**What Jesus has done:** "Because Jesus laid down his life for you, you can lay your life down for others by congratulating your teammates for their good game. I know that this is hard. But it was hard for Jesus to lay down his desires for you, too. He understands all you're going through right now. He'll give us both grace if we ask."
Gospel **Correction**	Deut. 4:9–14; Eph. 6:4; Titus 2:11–14	**Correcting him when he doubts or forgets:** "Right now you're acting like what Jesus has done for you doesn't matter. You're acting like winning is all there is. You know that even if you had won, you still wouldn't be truly satisfied, at least not for very long. God has given you and me an opportunity to be happy about what is really wonderful: his love. Your anger shows you how thankful you should be that you have a Savior."

Chart 5.1: "Of the Lord" Parenting *continued*

Category	Scripture	Example
Rehearsing Gospel **Promises** for both unbelieving and believing children	John 3:16–18; 8:24; Acts 16:31; Rom. 3:23–24; 4:22–25; 10:9–13	**If he isn't a Christian:** "I understand why you're so mad about not winning. It's because winning is all you have. Because you don't believe in Jesus's love for you, your whole life will be spent trying to win and never being satisfied. And then you'll have to stand before God, and all you'll have is your record of failure. Striking out isn't the worst thing that will ever happen to you. Living your life to win something other than Jesus is. But you can turn to him today."
		If he says he is a Christian: "Jesus Christ has paid the price for your sin. Jesus Christ has given you his perfect record. You are a new person with a new identity. Your new identity is that of a beloved child, not a failed baseball player. He'll never leave you nor forsake you. You can be confident that he will always hear you and give you grace and help. He will sustain you throughout your whole life and bring you home to be with him forever. Winning is nice, but having Jesus is better. I'm so glad that we can both look forward to a time when we won't make any more mistakes. Won't that be wonderful?"

Correction

Grace does not forbid us from correcting our children. But gospel correction reminds us to bring correction to them in the context of what Jesus has already done for them and his great love for them. Our angry and ashamed baseball player needs to repent not only of his anger and desire to approve of himself but also of desiring to be perfect on his own and of ignoring the perfection Jesus has provided for him in his justifying love. His anger is simply a symptom of a heart that desires to win rather than to be won.

Promises

Children need to be reminded of God's promises. They need to know the promises that he has made if they fail to believe that he is as merciful and good as he says he is. Failure and shame are all that await them. On the other hand, if they say that they believe, then they need to be reminded of the promises he has made to love and care for them, no matter how they fail.

Here are five simple words for you to take with you every day: Manage, Nurture, Train, Correct, and Promise. The beginning letters of these five categories are MNTCP. You probably know how making an acrostic can help you remember certain important facts. This is one that will help you remember these categories and will also remind you of one more very important aspect of your parenting—prayer (which we will look at in chapter 8). The acrostic can also stand for Moms Need To Constantly Pray.

In this chapter we've learned what the Bible has to say about how to raise our children. We've learned that there are different facets of "of the Lord" parenting and that what is called for in one situation may not be what is best in the next. Although just managing our children without giving them gospel truth never fulfills our entire obligation, many times that's all we've got time and energy for. Yes, there are plenty of times that simply call for managing a situation, but management is only one of our responsibilities. Here are some questions you can ask yourself, remembering this acrostic, Moms Need To Constantly Pray:

- Does this circumstance simply call for *management*?
- Now that the situation has calmed down, do I have an opportunity to *nurture* his soul with the gospel?
- Is this the time to *train* him in how to apply what Jesus has already done for him?
- Do I need to *correct* her attitudes or actions so that they are more in line with the good news?
- Should I remind him of God's *promises*, either of blessing for faith or of punishment for unbelief?
- Finally, is this just a time for me to *pray* and ask the Lord to show me how the gospel applies to my own heart? Do I need clarity to understand why my child is struggling or resisting right now? Do I need clarity into my heart's responses so that I am not sucked down into her unbelief, anger, and despair? What is it that bothers me about his attitude? Why?

Again, here are our five words used both ways: Manage, Nurture, Train, Correct, and Promise, and Moms Need To Constantly Pray. We've given you these five categories so that you can begin to expand your parenting to more accurately reflect the phrase, "in the Lord." But please take heart: remember that *we are not commanding you to try to do every single one of them every time you speak to your children.* Many times, and especially with younger children, all you're going to be able to do is manage them. We do want you to begin to pray that the Lord will help you remember to do more than that, but this isn't a new set of rules for you to follow. These are simply categories for you to begin to think and pray about.

Think Over What I Say

Although the apostle Paul did not have a wife or children (as far as we know), he did have Timothy, his son in the faith. What follows is part of the fatherly advice he gave to him. Can you see how he nurtured, trained, and corrected him in the Lord?

> *You then, my child, be strengthened by the grace that is in Christ Jesus.* . . . Share in suffering as a good soldier of Christ Jesus. No soldier gets entangled in civilian pursuits, since his aim is to please the one who enlisted him. An athlete is not crowned unless he competes according to the rules. It is the hard-working farmer who ought to have the first share of the crops. *Think over what I say*, for the Lord will give you understanding in everything. *Remember Jesus Christ*, risen from the dead, the offspring of David, as preached in my gospel, for which I am suffering, bound with chains as a criminal. (2 Tim. 2:1, 3–9)

Look again at that passage. Paul knew that only grace would strengthen his dear son. So, before he spoke to Timothy about the work he needed to do, he reminded him of grace. Yes, he is to work hard, suffering as a soldier, an athlete, a farmer. But Timothy's life is lived in a context. Sometimes it takes hard work and suffering in order to even begin to understand that context. What is that context? "Remember Jesus Christ, risen from the dead, the offspring of David, as preached in my gospel."

Paul's command to "bring them up in the discipline and instruction of the Lord" means this: that parents are to think about and remember Jesus Christ and then train their children to understand how everything in their life—their joys and sorrows, their trials and labors, their doubts, sin, and shame—is to be understood and approached in the light of Jesus Christ, who descended from David rather than from Levi, died, and rose from the dead. That is the best news any child could hear. Distinctly Christian parenting must be accomplished in the environment of the good news about Jesus Christ or it is not *Christian* parenting. It may work for a while, it may make your life manageable, and God may use it, but it is not "of the Lord."

As we close this chapter, let us nurture you with a soul-satisfying repast of grace from the Psalms:

> Bless the LORD, O my soul,
>> and all that is within me,
>> bless his holy name!
> Bless the LORD, O my soul,
>> and *forget not all his benefits*,
> who forgives all your iniquity,
>> who heals all your diseases,
> who redeems your life from the pit,
>> who crowns you with steadfast love and mercy,
> who satisfies you with good
>> so that your youth is renewed like the eagle's.
> The LORD works righteousness
>> and justice for all who are oppressed.
> He made known his ways to Moses,
>> his acts to the people of Israel.
> The LORD is merciful and gracious,
>> slow to anger and abounding in steadfast love.
> He will not always chide,
>> nor will he keep his anger forever.
> He does not deal with us according to our sins,
>> nor repay us according to our iniquities.
> For as high as the heavens are above the earth,
>> so great is his steadfast love toward those who fear him;
> as far as the east is from the west,
>> so far does he remove our transgressions from us.
> As a father shows compassion to his children,
>> so the LORD shows compassion to those who fear him.

For he knows our frame; he remembers that we are dust.

(Ps. 103:1–14)

Remembering God's Grace

Please don't ignore what the Holy Spirit might be doing in your heart through this chapter. Do take the time to think deeply about it and answer the questions.

1) How does grace train us? How can we use grace when training our children?
2) Has your understanding of bringing up children in the nurture and admonition *of the Lord* changed? How? What does that phrase mean?
3) Does it surprise you that there are only two direct commands about child training in the New Testament? How does this truth inform your parenting?
4) We highlighted five categories of gospel parenting: M _____ N_____ T_____ C_____ P_____. To help you remember these categories, we made another acrostic: "Moms Need To Constantly _____."
5) When we fail as parents, what is our only hope?
6) Summarize in three or four sentences what you have learned in this chapter.

6

Wisdom Greater Than Solomon's

Praise his name, our God is glorious in wisdom. Kings came to learn the wisdom of Solomon, but a greater than Solomon is here: Jesus Christ!
~ EDMUND P. CLOWNEY[1]

All their hopes had been trampled in the dust beneath the brutal heel of Rome's boot. For more than three years they had seen his miracles and heard his words. They had been convinced. Surely this was the "one to redeem Israel" (Luke 24:21). But then everything had gone terribly wrong. He had been arrested, beaten, crucified. He was dead, and with him went all their hopes.

It was the day after the Sabbath, Sunday, and life-as-usual had returned, as it always did, draped in shadows of hopelessness, futility, and confusion. *We thought we understood; we thought he was the One, the Messiah. How could we have been so mistaken?* So they began their sad trek together, up the road to Emmaus. They had no idea what awaited them on that road and how it would change everything they thought they knew.

While it was true that the Lord Jesus had died, and it had been days since he had been laid in Joseph's cold tomb, he was no longer held by death's grip. No, he was out walking on the road. He was intercepting his grieving uncle Cleopas and perhaps his aunt Mary too.[2] His dear grieving friends needed something from him that would forever dispel their sadness and illumine their understanding. As they walked along the road, Jesus himself "drew near and went with them" (Luke 24:15). He asked them what they were discussing, and upon hearing their sorrow and confusion he gradually opened their minds to understand the real meaning of the Old Testament Scriptures—*they were all about him* (John 5:39). Here is how Luke describes their experience:

> Beginning with Moses and all the Prophets, [Jesus] interpreted to them in all the Scriptures the things concerning himself. . . . They said to each other, "Did not our hearts burn within us while he talked to us on the road, while he opened to us the Scriptures?" . . . Then he said to them, "These are my words that I spoke to you while I was still with you, that everything written about me in the Law of Moses and the Prophets and the Psalms must be fulfilled." Then he opened their minds to understand the Scriptures. (Luke 24:27, 32, 44–45)

In essence, Jesus was teaching them that "all truths come to their realization in relation to [him]."[3] When he referenced "the Law of Moses and the Prophets and the Psalms," he wasn't limiting his meaning to those specific books. He meant the entire Old Testament. Every passage of Scripture and, in fact, every occurrence in all of creation has its fulfillment in Jesus Christ. "All things were created through him and for him . . . that in everything he might be preeminent," Paul wrote (Col. 1:16, 18; see also Heb. 1:3–4). Jesus stands at the forefront of absolutely everything as preeminent Lord over all.

Right about now you might be wondering why we've taken you on this jaunt up the Emmaus road to eavesdrop on a conversation, when this is supposed to be a book about parenting. The reason is that we're about to wade into the wisdom of the proverbs, and we want you to understand how to read them in the light of the gospel of grace. We want you to see that the proverbs (and indeed, all of Scripture) are preeminently about Jesus's death, resurrection, and entrance into his glory (Luke 24:26). It is the Lord himself who teaches us to read the proverbs asking this question: "Where is my Savior?"[4]

Seeing Jesus in the Proverbs

For the most part, the proverbs were written by Solomon, the wisest man of his time (1 Kings 4:29–34), and although they are right and true words, not even Solomon was able to employ them in such a way that his own son wasn't foolish. Nevertheless, the proverbs were written to instill skill in the art of godly living in those who heed their counsel. Many are written as the words of a father to his son. Others are directed to parents as they seek to instill wisdom into their children.

If we approach the proverbs believing that the entire Bible "whispers his name,"[5] if we come with open eyes, looking for our Savior, we'll easily identify him there as the Wise Son. Yes, the proverbs do tell us how to live godly lives, but they also tell us about him. For instance, the command, "My son, if sinners entice you, do not consent," was abundantly fulfilled in Jesus's resistance to Satan's temptations in the wilderness. Jesus is the Wise Son who always did what was pleasing to his Father (Isa. 52:13; John 8:29). And although the Bible is nearly silent on Jesus's childhood, we do have this one description: "Jesus increased in wisdom and in stature and in favor with God and man" (Luke 2:52). He was completely obedient because he was fully wise, and he was loved by his Father and his parents. Jesus even refers to himself as the personification of wisdom (Matt. 11:19), while Paul assures us that in him are hidden *all* the treasures of wisdom and knowledge (Col. 2:3). Jesus is the denouement of Proverbs' Wise Son.

But Jesus isn't merely the Wise Son who gladdens his Father's heart (Prov. 10:1; Matt. 3:17). He is also the Son who feels the rod of correction meant for fools. He is the one whom the Roman guards received "with blows" (Mark 14:65). Although he was wise, the "rod of discipline," designed to drive folly away, was laid upon his bloody back (Prov. 26:3; Matt. 27:28–31). When the Holy Spirit opens our eyes to Jesus's presence, we see him everywhere in Proverbs. Here is a man with a wisdom greater and deeper than Solomon's (Matt. 12:42) who was treated like the fool who deserves a beating.

Jesus's identity as *the Wise Son who received blows* helps us understand how to apply the proverbs in our parenting. Remembering that Proverbs and the way we discipline are preeminently about Jesus Christ will transform the way we apply correction to our own children. And even in times of correction we'll whisper his name to them through our tears and theirs.

All of this is not to suggest that we ignore the plain teaching of Proverbs and instead simply look for Jesus. No, the plain words of the proverbs are for our good, and we will grow in wisdom if we respond to them in faith and humility. It is just that if we neglect to see Jesus there too, we will wrongly assume that we will be able to automatically accomplish something that not even Solomon could accomplish: produce wise children. In addition, because the proverbs are so clear-cut and seem like promises, we'll believe that our performance will guarantee success. Many so-called Christian parenting books develop the parental wisdom in Proverbs without any recognition of the presence of the Christ. Because a devout Jew could employ Proverbs in the same way, this isn't a Christian paradigm. Parenting methods that assume or ignore the gospel are not Christian. The gospel must hold the center in all we think, do, and say with our kids.

Physical Discipline and the Gospel

Proverbs enjoins the appropriate and loving use of physical force, what it calls "the rod," or spanking. Here are the four passages from Proverbs (and one from Hebrews) where we find commands to discipline with physical correction the children we love:[6]

> Whoever spares the rod hates his son, but he who loves him is diligent to discipline him. (Prov. 13:24)

> Folly is bound up in the heart of a child, but the rod of discipline drives it far from him. (Prov. 22:15)

> Do not withhold discipline from a child; if you strike him with a rod, he will not die. If you strike him with the rod, you will save his soul from Sheol. (Prov. 23:13–14)

> The rod and reproof give wisdom, but a child left to himself brings shame to his mother. (Prov. 29:15)

> For what son is there whom his father does not discipline? . . . We have had earthly fathers who disciplined us. . . . For they disciplined us for a short time as it seemed best to them. . . . For the moment all discipline seems painful rather than pleasant. (Heb. 12:7–11)

Every parent has to come to his or her own conclusion about physical discipline. Although many sincere Christians disagree, we believe that the Bible clearly teaches that corporal punishment is a sign of loving relationship. But even here, correction or punishment must come in the context of the Wise Son who took blows meant for fools. Here's how a conversation before or after a time of discipline might sound:

> David, I am grieved that you decided to disobey me when I clearly told you that it was time to put away your toys and get ready for supper. Because you blatantly defied my request and continued to play, even though you knew we were waiting for you, now I have to discipline you. You know that God commands me to train you to obey, and if I fail to discipline you now, I will be disobeying him. I am sad that I have to cause you pain. I know that you are sad too. I pray that you will understand that disobedience always causes pain. In fact, our disobedience caused the pain that Jesus felt on the cross, even though he had always perfectly obeyed and didn't deserve to be punished. He willingly took the punishment you and I deserve because he loves us. He stood in your place and felt the rod of correction too, so that we would never have to experience God's wrath. But I have to discipline you now because your disobedience shows me that you have forgotten how wonderful his love is. Instead of remembering how he loves you, you tried to make yourself happy on your own, without him, by disobeying me.
>
> If you believe that he has loved you and received punishment for you, then this kind of punishment will help remind you to live wisely, and the pain of it will soon be gone. But if you don't believe in his great goodness, then the punishment you receive today will be just the beginning of a lifetime of pain. Today, you can ask for forgiveness, and I will forgive you, and if you ask him, so will the Lord. But if you wait, if you harden your heart and refuse to change, then a day will come when it will be too late to ask for forgiveness. I am going to pray for you now, and then, later, if the Holy Spirit is moving in your heart to make you truly sorry for disobeying me, I promise I'll forgive you if you ask. Don't forget that the Lord has promised that everyone who calls on him will be saved. David, I love you, and I pray that you will call on him now, while you still can, and that this discipline will teach you that pain always follows disobedience.

Can you see how the gospel made a difference in the tone and content of that time of discipline? Of course, not every conversation should be exactly like that, nor does it need to be that lengthy. This isn't a script to be memorized but rather a model to encourage you to know how to exalt Jesus Christ even during a time of loving discipline of your children. As you pray for wisdom and ask the Holy Spirit to remind you of the suffering and exaltation of Jesus, you'll find that your heart is warmed to the gospel too, helping you discover the sweetness of the gospel when you have to suffer discipline yourself.

The good news teaches us that the record of the Wise Son has been given to believing children—and that doesn't change even during times of discipline. Although some children compound their sin during discipline by being stubbornly angry or sullen, they can be reassured that Jesus suffered through his time of punishment perfectly, without sinning and that this is their record if they truly believe. Times of correction are to be times of gospel witness, reminding children that Jesus knows what it is to be punished and that he submitted to it even though he didn't deserve it.

Is This Sin or Weakness and Immaturity?

Of course, before we use physical correction, we need to be sure that our children understand what we're asking of them and that they are capable of obeying. Perhaps their disobedience is a matter of immaturity or weakness. Paul wrote, "When I was a child, I spoke like a child, I thought like a child, I reasoned like a child. When I became a man, I gave up childish ways" (1 Cor. 13:11). Our children have "childish ways" because they are not adults. They speak, think, and reason like children because they are children. Their childish ways may be sinful, or they may be evidence of weakness or inability to think ahead, to weigh consequences, to manage their time, to remember what they were supposed to be doing, to say the right thing.

There is a difference between childishness and foolishness. One is the result of normal immaturity. The other is the result of sin. While we want to be diligent to train our children so that they mature into responsible adulthood and give up their childish ways, careful thought needs to be given as to whether their actions are the fruit of willful defiance or weak childishness. Does this disobedience call for physical correction, or might this be a time to be sure that the child is capable of obedience?

When a two-year-old continues to try to touch something he shouldn't touch (for whatever reason), his parent should move his hand and tell him no. Perhaps he could be given something else to play with instead. Toddlers don't need explanations. They simply need to be kept from danger and taught to obey Mom's and Dad's voices. This outward management does not transform the heart or make them more receptive to grace. We don't have that kind of power over their hearts. It simply teaches them how to obey outwardly—if they respond.

If our little toddler continues to try to grab the object or falls down on the ground crying because he is being denied, the level of correction should be stepped up. Along with a stern no, a firm slap on his hand or on his bottom is appropriate.[7] He is not old enough to understand all the ramifications of his disobedience. He is still thinking and reasoning like a child. He simply has to begin to learn to obey those in authority over him. He should then be hugged and sent along to play again. This is the kind of training that falls into the *management* category we talked about in chapter 5. If we manage our children in this way while they are very young, frequently we'll find that the necessity for physical correction lessens as they mature. Some children are very compliant and learn quickly to move their hand in another direction when Mommy says no. Others are more resistant and need the same lesson over and over again.

Depending on the maturity of the child, time spent in gospel instruction (nurturing, training, correction, giving promises) should begin to increase even as the need for actual physical correction decreases. The more a child understands and believes the gospel, the more we are able to reason with him instead of spanking him. Personally, I (Jessica) have seen the Holy Spirit crush my son's proud heart more deeply than a spanking ever could. Our goal is always to get to the point where we are talking with our kids about the truth of the gospel more and more, believing that their training will be better brought about by the conviction of the Holy Spirit instead of the rod. We can learn that our children are moving toward maturity when it doesn't take a spanking to start them in the direction of repentance.

Sometimes we may feel that we are in a season in which we are doing nothing but giving spanks and that when we share the gospel with our kids, they act as though they're deaf. Sometimes it is months before we see any fruit from all our efforts. When it's wintertime in their souls, that is the time we need to continue to obey in faith, believing that the Lord will use our efforts to bless our children, reciting the gospel over and over to ourselves, and waiting and praying for the life-giving work of the Holy Spirit.[8]

Our Welcome in the Family

We know that some parents insist that children immediately ask for forgiveness for their offenses, sometimes so that the correction will cease. Although such parents long for immediate reconciliation and repentance, we disagree with this practice. We do not think it is ever advisable to tempt children to lie. Certainly children should be taught that pain is a consequence for disobedience and that their disobedience affects others, not just themselves. They should be encouraged to ask God and others (including their parents) for forgiveness, but only if they are genuinely sorry.

If we encourage children to ask for forgiveness when their hearts haven't been stricken by the rod of the Holy Spirit's conviction, we are training them to be hypocritical. We are inadvertently teaching them that false professions of sorrow will satisfy God. God is never pleased with outward proclamations of devotion when the heart is far from him (Isa. 29:13; Matt. 15:7–9); in fact, he hates it. The truth is that we can never know with any certainty whether their proclamations of repentance are true, because only God knows the heart (Jer. 17:5). Assuming that we can see into the heart is a sign of our pride, and it is dangerous for them.

Rather than insisting on an immediate show of repentance, you should give your children time to respond to the prompting of the Holy Spirit. Assure them you are praying for them. Ask them to wait for a while, pray that they will have grace to understand and change, and then leave them in the hands of the Holy Spirit. When you do, you'll be amazed at how quickly many of them will come around and willingly ask for forgiveness. But even if they don't, you can and should continue to lavish them with your love, confessing your own unbelief, disobedience, and faith in God's promise to continue to love you even though you don't see or confess even one tenth of your own sin.

We don't have to sever our relationship with unrepentant children, because our relationship is not based on their merit but rather on the ties of family love. All our relationships are based on and must reflect our relationship with the Lord. Our sin does grieve us but, if we are in Christ, our sin can never separate us from him. "God does not slack his promises because of our sins," says Paul, in essence, "or hasten them because of our righteousness and merits. He pays no attention to either."[9]

We are not telling you to ignore bad behavior; nor are we saying that sinful behavior should not be corrected. We are saying that we should teach our children that sinful behavior does not alter their relationship with us. If our parenting is modeled on the gospel, then their sin, hardness, and unbelief will grieve us, we will seek to discipline and correct it, we will pray for them about it, and we will continue to love and welcome them in spite of it. But we will not demand a *show* of repentance before we welcome them back into relationship.

Remembering that genuine love for God and others will *only* grow in the environment of his initiating love for us will help us when we are fearful and are tempted to demand some show of repentance to ease our concerns. As they struggle with true repentance and godly sorrow, we can calm our anxious hearts by remembering these precious words from Martin Luther:

> Because we have only the first fruits of the Spirit, and the remnants of sin still remain in us, we do not obey the law perfectly. But this imperfection is not imputed to us who are in Christ [who] has blessed us. . . . *We are nourished and tenderly cherished for Christ's sake, in the lap of God's longsuffering.*[10]

Beautiful, comforting words! Nourish and tenderly cherish your children in the lap of your longsuffering and entrust them into the hands of a faithful Savior, who alone has the ability to transform the heart. Although as parents we long for some assurance that our children are responding, that we are doing the right thing, we don't need to do his work for him. He was able to save your soul. He is able to save theirs, too. "Grace frees us from having to earn God's acceptance by meeting others' expectations, and it also frees us from the unholy pride and prejudice of determining others' acceptance by God on the basis of our own wisdom."[11]

You Are My Beloved Child, Now Act Like It

Covenant Theological Seminary president Bryan Chapell reflects on the shift in his own parenting as he began to be touched by the truths of grace:

> I used to say to my son, "Colin, because of what you did you are a bad boy." I would characterize him by his actions. But then I recognized that this is not the way that God treats me. The grace that identifies me as God's child is not based on my actions. He characterizes me based on my relationship with him,

not on the basis of what I have done. My union with Christ (the indicative of who I am) precedes and motivates my obedience (the imperative). Thus, to treat our children as God treats us, my wife and I put ourselves under the discipline of saying to our son, "Colin, don't do that, because you are my child." In essence, we urged our son, "Be what you are, our beloved," rather than, "Do, so you will be beloved."[12]

This is the pattern for training in obedience that we find all throughout the Scriptures. For example, in 1 Thessalonians 5:5–11 Paul does this very thing. He tells the Thessalonian believers that they are "children of light, of the day" (1 Thess. 5:5). He tells them who they are not, children "of the night or of the darkness" (v. 5). After reminding them of their identity, he tells them how to live: soberly, with faith, love, and hope. Then *again* he reminds them of their status before the Father: they are not "destined . . . for wrath, but to obtain salvation through our Lord Jesus Christ" (v. 9). Then *again* he reminds them of the good news: Jesus Christ is the one who "died for us" so that we would live with him, *again* reminding them of relationship (v. 10). Finally, he tells them to encourage and build up one another with these words (v. 11).[13] If you want your parenting to be based on the Bible, *this must be the ruling model for it*. Remind your children who they are, of your love and welcome. Then remind them of God's gracious offer of salvation through faith in Jesus Christ. *Then* command their obedience.

Proverbs directs advice toward sons at least twenty-three times.[14] We see a father pleading with his son to take to heart the training he is giving him: "Hear, my son, your father's instruction, and forsake not your mother's teaching" (Prov. 1:8ff.; see also 2:1; 3:1; 4:10, 20; 5:1; 6:20; 7:1; 19:27; 23:19). He appeals to him to live wisely and thereby comfort his father's heart and make it glad: "My son, if your heart is wise, my heart too will be glad. My inmost being will exult when your lips speak what is right" (Prov. 23:15–16). This is no detached training from a drill sergeant. This father has anchored his gladness in his son's wisdom, much like John does in 3 John 4: "I have no greater joy than to hear that my children are walking in the truth." The father in Proverbs goes so far as to entreat his son to give him his heart and invites him into his life, to learn by observing his ways (Prov. 23:26). This is training in a loving, committed relationship.

These parents (both father and mother) train their child in wise living.[15] They tell him the folly of entering into immorality, of laziness, of stubbornness, of mismanaging resources, of living as though there were no sovereign God who deserved respect. These commands are given to the son in the context of his relationship with both father and mother. Solomon, the father, is appealing to his son to remember the love that his son has received and to react in kind. "You are my dearly beloved son; please remember who you already are and act like it."

Donkeys, Carrots, and Sticks

Everyone struggles with obedience no matter how old they are. Little children want to touch what Daddy has said no to; older children refuse to share their toys even though they know they should; teens sneak their cell phones out to text their friends when they should be studying; adults know they are commanded to love their neighbor but gossip about him anyway. No matter what our age or our maturity in Christ, everyone has a problem with sin, even the apostle Paul. He said, "I do not do the good I want, but the evil I do not want is what I keep on doing" (Rom. 7:19).

Every parent also has a theory of training and motivation, an underlying belief of how to get kids to do what they want, whether it's clearly stated or not. During the 1800s one theory based on promises of reward and threats of punishment was developed. Basically, this theory proposed that there were two ways to get a donkey to move a cart. First, you could dangle a carrot in front of the donkey, fooling the donkey into thinking that if he pulls the cart far enough, he'll get to eat the carrot. The second is to prod the donkey along the road by hitting him with a stick. If the donkey is motivated by the ultimate reward of a carrot, the stick won't be necessary, but if he's not really all that interested in carrots, then the stick will be employed. Either way, through reward or through punishment, the cart driver gets what he wants.

I learned this motivational paradigm when I taught in a Christian school in the 1970s and early 1980s. I remember a cartoon of a silly-looking donkey moseying down the road with a carrot dangling in front of his dim eyes and a farmer seated behind him with a whip. It seemed logical to me. Motivate the kids with a reward or motivate them with punishment; either way was fine, as long as they got down the road.

I'm sorry to say that I carried this philosophy over into my home with my own children. When they behaved, they got to put beans in a jar to earn a trip to the ice cream shop. When they failed to behave, beans were removed. If one child disobeyed, the others suffered for it and would pressure the rebel to fall into line. I really believed that the carrots and the sticks were working well with my little donkeys. But there were several significant problems: my children weren't donkeys; they were image bearers of the incarnate God; I wasn't ultimately in charge—he was—and, of course, we had completely overlooked the gospel.

How would the gospel transform the motivational paradigm above? Quite simply, by turning the entire model on its head. Because both parents and children obstinately refuse to pull the cart of God's glory down the road, the Father broke the stick of punishment on his obedient Son's back. Rather than trying to entice us by dangling an unattainable carrot of perfect welcome and forgiveness incessantly in front of our faces, God the Father freely feeds the carrot to us, his enemies. He simply moves outside all our categories for reward and punishment, for human motivation, and gives us all the reward and takes upon himself all the punishment. He lavishes grace upon grace on us and bears in his own person all the wrath that we deserve. Then he tells us, in light of all that he's done, "Obey."

Yes, we do have promises of rewards in heaven, but these are not earned by us through our merit. Yes, there are promises of punishment, but not for those who are "in Christ." All our punishment has been borne by him. The carrot is ours. The stick is his. Manage them with beans in a jar if you must, but be sure to tell them that it isn't the gospel. And perhaps, once in a while, just fill the jar up with beans and take everyone out for ice cream, and when your son asks you, "Daddy, why do we get ice cream? How did the jar get to be full?" you'll know what to say, won't you?

Deeper Wisdom from the Proverbs

As we close our time thinking about the proverbs, here are two more verses to help you wrestle through what we've said. The first is Proverbs 16:7: "When a man's ways please the LORD, he makes even his enemies to be at peace with him." How would you explain this verse to your children? We hope that you wouldn't tell them that God promises to make people like them if they behave. Instead, you might say something more like this: "When you live in the light of the wisdom God gives, you'll usually find that people will treat you well." But it's best if, after you have said that, you add, "Although that's true, we also know that Jesus's ways pleased the Lord, but his enemies killed him. And that's not all. By his sacrifice he made his enemies (you and me) his friends! We're at peace with him right now because he bore all the wrath that we deserved. Isn't that good news?"

Here's one final proverb: "He who justifies the wicked and he who condemns the righteous are both alike an abomination to the LORD" (Prov. 17:15). If we fail to see the Wise Son who received blows meant for a fool, we'll miss the depth of this wisdom. Of course, having righteous judgment pleases God. But Jesus is the one who justifies the wicked. The Father is the one who condemned the righteous. Why? So that we would no longer be the wicked, so that we would move out of our tit-for-tat world and into the grace of the gospel of Jesus Christ, and so that we would be overwhelmed with his wisdom and bathe our dear children in it every day.

Remembering God's Grace

Please don't ignore what the Holy Spirit might be doing in your heart through this chapter. Do take the time to think deeply about it and answer the questions.

1) What are the proverbs meant to be in our lives?

2) Why do we discipline our children? What is the goal?

3) What is the difference between sin and immaturity? Have you expected too much maturity from your children?

4) Do you rely on methods or on the Holy Spirit to change your child's heart? Do you even think about heart change, or are you consumed only with getting them to obey?

5) Do you ever treat your children differently or hold them at arm's length after you have disciplined them? Do you welcome them back into loving relationship freely or begrudgingly?

6) What method do you tend to default to when feeling hopeless in your parenting: reward or punishment? How does the gospel change the way we discipline?
7) How does our treasuring the gospel help our children?
8) Summarize in three or four sentences what you have learned in this chapter.

7

The One Good Story

All the gifts which we possess have been bestowed by God and entrusted to us on condition that they be distributed for our neighbors' benefit.
~ JOHN CALVIN[1]

When a stranger sojourns with you in your land, you shall not do him wrong. You shall treat the stranger who sojourns with you as the native among you, and you shall love him as yourself, for you were strangers in the land of Egypt: I am the LORD your God.
~ LEVITICUS 19:33–34

Imagine this: a great King sends his beloved Son to sojourn in the land he owns. Rather than loving this stranger, the natives of the land do him wrong. They do not love him; they do not remember that they were strangers who have been loved. No, instead they kill him. They forget all the great King's commands, yet he blesses and forgives them and raises up his beloved Son to ensure that they, the real strangers in this story, would be blessed and cared for forever. Generous mercy like this is simply unbelievable apart from God's grace.

~

Andrew was at the door again, which wasn't unusual because their home had become this little guy's home away from home. Andrew came from an unbelieving family, and his parents were gone more than they were home, leaving him in the "care" of his sixteen-year-old sister, who spent all her time on the phone and watching MTV. Andrew was rough; he used inappropriate language, told unsavory jokes far beyond his short life, and had never been introduced to any form of morality, let alone gospel Christianity. When the mother heard his voice, she cringed; then she remembered the gospel story and prayed for wisdom and grace.

~

Many of Mark's teammates from Little League were attending a sleepover at the coach's house. Pizza, games, and Star Wars movies were on the agenda. Mark had asked if he could go. Mark's dad and mom were concerned about some of the content in a few of the *Star Wars* movies and about Mark spending the night with so many unbelieving children. Was this one of those instances when Mark's family should stand against the world, or could this be a door to teach Mark how to interact with it? Although Mark was homeschooled, the family had purposely put him in Little League so that the family would have the opportunity to intermingle with unsaved people.[2] What would gospel wisdom look like in this circumstance?

~

Little six-year-old Megan was filled with dreams of being a princess and having a wonderful prince come and marry her. She dressed up in her princess dresses, tiaras, and slippers all the time and continually played like she was a beautiful princess, sometimes when she was supposed to be cleaning her room or helping her mother. When her friends came over, they all dressed up together, and her mom wondered if Megan's imaginary world was harmful, especially since it was obvious she was missing the point that Jesus called her to be a servant, not a princess. Should she restrict her from wearing her princess clothes?

~

Luke is a teenager who loves his music and plays his guitar whenever he gets a chance. Both his mom and dad have tried to be understanding about Luke's choices in music, but they find that they've grown really tired of it. Up until now he has listened only to music produced by supposed Christians, even though his parents aren't sure the words have anything to do with God at all. But now, he has taken an interest in a new band that has no Christian pretense at all. The lyrics to the songs don't seem to be much different from what he has been listening to all along, but his parents wonder if this is the beginning of a slide down a slippery slope. What should they say? Should they stop him from listening even though they don't think there's anything terribly wrong with the music, or should they say yes and then open the door to the possibility that he will want to listen to more and more?

Answers from the Gospel

What does the story of the beloved Son who died and was raised have to do with lost neighbors, questionable entertainment, little princesses, and music-loving teens? Every parent knows what it is like to have to make decisions about the clothing, hairstyles, entertainment, and relationships of their children. If there were a place where a tidy list of do's and don'ts would fit nicely, this would be it. It would be very easy for us to say, "Keep your children from every outside influence," and simply leave the matter there. But you know us well enough by now to know that isn't what we're going to do. We refuse to give you more law to impose on your children, because the law doesn't breed obedience and love. It produces only pride and despair—for you and them—and it won't ever produce the joy that is to be our strength. So instead of giving you a catalog of do's and don'ts, we're going to help you learn how to approach every decision with the one good story, the gospel story, in mind (see Appendix 1: The One Good Story).

We know that this won't be as easy as giving you a list to go by, at least not at first, but it will encourage dependence on the Holy Spirit and nourish the entire family's souls. So, as an introduction to get your thinking going in the right direction, here are a few questions to consider when you are faced with a decision that isn't clearly spelled out in Scripture:

- What does the gospel teach me about this choice?
- Where do I see the great King in this situation?
- What does the activity of the beloved Son teach me about this?
- Is this a trick of the wicked Imposter?
- What am I believing when I forbid or allow this?

- Is my allowance of this choice a function of love for God or love for the world, or is it something else entirely?
- Am I remembering the Great Commandment to love my neighbor and seeking to fulfill the Great Commission to share the gospel with him as part of a relationship?
- Am I building a fortress of piety in an effort to keep the bad out and the good in? Or am I naively inviting the wicked Imposter into my family?

Do those questions seem too complex? If so, please know that you don't need to remember every single one all the time. This isn't a formula for you to memorize so that you don't make any mistakes and so that your children turn out perfectly. Rather, it is simply a way to reframe your thinking; it's a way to immerse yourself and your children in the good news.

If you try to remember that you have a loving heavenly Father, who sent his beloved Son into the world to undo all the sadness and deception that the wicked Imposter has brought, you'll be headed in the right direction. If you remember what the Lord Jesus has already done for you, your family, and your unbelieving neighbors, and if you ask the Holy Spirit for help, you'll find that these kinds of decisions are more easily made. Even if you don't remember to ask them, even if you make a decision without thinking about the gospel, the Lord is faithful to use everything in your life for your good and his glory.

So Many Opinions

We're well aware that there is a great diversity of opinion about how to make wise decisions and that it is precisely in such decisions that our attachment to the law shows up most glaringly. Because of parents' loving desire to protect their children from the evil in the world, some parents live more like reclusive monks than like first-century Christians who were famous for their love for and service within their cities—cities that in many cases were more overtly wicked than cities found in modern-day America.

In the two cities to which Paul wrote his parental directives, Ephesus and Colossae, goddess worship, temple prostitution, superstition, sorcery, abortion, infanticide, and child slavery were commonplace. These cities more closely resembled a casino on the Las Vegas strip than a little house on the prairie. In the midst of all this filth and degradation, Paul did not command parents to remove their children from these cities and flee to the suburbs to raise them in an environment more conducive to holiness. Sure, there were reclusive sects in the ancient Near East, but they were insignificant, definitely not those that turned the world upside down. How could they have been? They shunned interaction with the world and with the people who lived there.

On the other hand, we know that some parents are so foolishly cavalier about what they expose their children to that they acquaint them with every sort of base influence, having not taken time to discern their child's inability to understand or resist the deceptions within them. They pay no attention to even secular ratings on video games, music, or movies, fearing that their children will resent their interference and their restricting them from what all their friends enjoy. Surely the Lord who invited little children up onto his lap would not want them thrown into the cesspool that many of their peers swim in.

There is great diversity among all sincere believers regarding what are commonly called "wisdom issues," so let's try to discern wisdom by examining the Scriptures through the lenses of the one good story, the gospel.

Come Out from Among Them

It is interesting to note that parents are nowhere specifically commanded to keep their children secluded from the people of the world. The verses that come closest to doing this are those concerning the marriage of Israelites to unbelieving Gentiles:

> You shall make no covenant with them and show no mercy to them. You shall not intermarry with them, giving your daughters to their sons or taking their daughters for your sons, for they would turn away your sons from following me, to serve other gods. (Deut. 7:2–4)[3]

Under the old covenant, the law about marriage was so significant that the exiles who returned to Israel after the Babylonian captivity were actually commanded to divorce their pagan wives. Because fathers usually arranged marriages for their children (both sons and daughters), this command forbade them from doing so, with some gloriously gracious exceptions.[4] This law concerned primarily the national purity of Israel, but there was also a spiritual component. The Lord wanted his children's hearts to be free from the worship of the idols of the nations that surrounded them, and living intimately with an idolater would create unnecessary temptation and discord.

This law against such entanglement with unbelieving neighbors is recast in an interesting way in the New Testament. Whereas the Old Testament saints were forbidden from marrying Gentiles and returning exiles were even commanded to divorce them, the Corinthians who came to faith after marrying were not commanded to divorce their unbelieving partners. In fact, Paul says that the believing partner's influence in the home set the unbeliever apart from "other unbelievers and from the evil of the world."[5] Because of the intimate marital relationship, the believer was in a position to bless the unbeliever through the daily demonstration of his or her faith.[6]

In another well-known passage, 2 Corinthians 6:14–16, Paul warns believers against being "unequally yoked" with unbelievers. This passage has broad implications—Paul was not speaking *specifically* about marriage here, or even about avoiding worldly influences. Paul was labeling as "unbelievers" those who had resisted him from *within* the congregation, those who had said they were believers but did not submit to his apostolic authority.[7]

More broadly, Christian children and their parents are clearly warned against being "yoked together" or allied with those who oppose Christ's authority in the church in such a way that the "unbeliever" has the power to strongly direct, control, or influence the believer. Paul here is referring to people *within* the local church who were masquerading as believers, not unbelievers outside the church. Associations with unbelievers outside the church are not to be shunned (1 Cor. 5:10) but rather to be undertaken, albeit with discernment and caution.

This interpretation of these two passages from 1 and 2 Corinthians harmonizes beautifully with the story of the beloved Son, doesn't it? When we consider his mission, his total immersion within our sinful world, we can see how he does not call us away from unbelievers but rather to follow him into relationship with them. He sees our influence upon them as a sanctifying force for his glory. This is the principle clearly demonstrated by Jesus's blatant disregard of the clean/unclean distinctions when touching lepers (Matt. 8:3) and the dead (Mark 5:41; Luke 7:14). To the Lord Jesus, a promiscuous half-breed Samaritan woman was not unclean (John 4:9). She was a scorched soul who needed a drink of his life-transforming living water. He associated with sinners and tax collectors (Matt. 9:10–11; 11:19; Luke 15:1) and by doing so infuriated those who prided themselves on their separation from the world and punctilious law keeping. His holiness rubbed off on them rather than the other way around. His presence in our sinful world did not pollute his holiness. Rather, he identified with us for the very purpose that he would make us holy.

This message of integration rocked the early Jewish church to their core. Peter himself needed a shocking visit from God to overcome his prejudice against those outside the family of faith, even though he had spent years watching Jesus's interaction with Gentiles and sinners. Here is Peter's testimony about his change of heart: "You yourselves know how unlawful it is for a Jew to associate with or to visit anyone of another nation, but God has shown me that I should not call any person common or unclean" (Acts 10:28; see also Rom. 14:14; 1 Cor. 5:9–10).

It's very important to notice that the "unlawful" associations Peter referenced here were not restrictions imposed by the Lord. No, they were actually mere Jewish tradition, a legalistic and heartless fencing off of the nation from those around her to preserve her purity. In an effort to be "super holy," the Pharisees had expanded God's prohibitions about mixture in marriage and worship to forbid any association with unbelievers at all. Peter had been taught not to "associate with" or "visit" anyone who was not Jewish. *This was never God's plan for his people.* That Peter really had to struggle against his conscience in this is obvious by his failure to remember it later in Antioch (Gal. 2:11–14). Paul violently opposed Peter's misguided exclusivity in the strongest way: he said it was "not in step with the truth of the gospel" (Gal. 2:14).

Peter had to learn that God had never commanded his people to disassociate from unbelievers. No, rather, they had been ordained to be a blessing to unbelievers. The commissioning of the early church in Acts 1:8 includes taking this good news to every part of the earth, outside our little family circle, especially into our neighborhoods. Let's face it: it's impossible to be a witness to unbelieving neighbors if we shun them because we are afraid they will pollute our holy family.

So, let all the unbelieving Andrews come over. Yes, they will need to be told about appropriate behavior. Yes, they're absolutely clueless about grace and gratitude. Of course you'll have to keep a closer eye on your kids while Andrew is there, and you'll have to talk with your kids about the lostness of their new friend, but a neighborhood full of little unbelievers is a marvelous mission field! Your home and your children may be the only witness of true gospel Christianity they have ever seen. Again, you'll have to be careful that your children are not coming under the control or strong influence of unbelievers, that they aren't committing to a relationship with them in any way other than for friendly gospel witness and service, but the possibilities for gospel-driven relationships are simply limitless.[8]

Here are a few questions to ask yourself as you construct a framework for your children's relating to your lost neighbors:

- Is a particular neighborhood child simply unchurched, or is he churched and rebellious?
- Does this neighborhood child seem to hold a strong influence over my child that I should protect him from?
- Is my child mature enough to articulate proper boundaries and gospel truths to a particular neighborhood child?
- Does my child love the Savior, or is he a rebel looking for someone to rebel with?
- Is this a situation in which to remember the beloved Son or the wicked Imposter?
- Is this a safe time to allow my child the possibility of making a mistake in his choices?

These questions reflect the glories of the beloved Son and the tragedy of the wicked Imposter's lies. We don't want to play into his deception by allowing children who are still weak and immature to fall under the sway of a powerful, unbelieving friend. On the other hand, we don't want to believe our enemy's deceptions and fail to witness to and love those that Jesus brings to us. The possibility of sin is present on both sides of this problem, and Satan doesn't care which side we err on.

Sleepovers with Unbelievers—and Luke Skywalker

Another passage that is often used to bolster arguments for a more secluded family life is 1 Corinthians 15:33: "Do not be deceived: 'Bad company ruins good morals.'" This quotation about the evils of bad company is not taken from any passage in the Old Testament; it may be a quote from a secular source.[9] Paul's point in using this quotation is summed up well in Eugene Peterson's paraphrase, *The Message*: "Don't let yourselves be poisoned by this anti-resurrection loose talk. 'Bad company ruins good manners.'" Paul was warning about the dangers of association with those within the church who deny the resurrection. He was not making a comment about whether children of believers should associate with unbelieving children.

However, it's obvious that we become like those we most closely associate with. Proverbs 13:20 teaches us, "Whoever walks with the wise becomes wise, but the companion of fools will suffer harm." As Mark's parents seek to discern gospel wisdom, here are some questions they might consider:

- Is Mark overly influenced by any one boy on the team?
- Does Mark have other believing friends, or at least friends from Christian homes whom he spends most of his time with? In other words, does he spend most of his time walking with and under the influence of the wise?
- Is he able to resist the pull of the world when he's on the bench with his teammates?
- Do you notice a marked difference in his attitude after the games or practices?
- Does he see that being with his teammates is to be a purposeful time of trying to show them the gospel through his love, service, and humility? Or is he trapped by trying to fit in?

Let's assume that Mark seems able to keep his head on straight when he's with the team, so you think the sleepover is something you will allow. But that's not the only decision you need to make. You also have to decide whether to let him watch the *Star Wars* movies. Again, this is an area of great divergence of opinion among sincere believers. Rather than try to build a case either for or against all media, we want you to think through these issues in light of the gospel.

We want our children to know and believe the one good story. Every other story is a copy or shadow of this one. Some copies of it are quite good and shout the truth. Others speak only the faintest whisper of it or, by its absence, remind us of the truth. We want our kids to know the one good story so well that when they see Luke Skywalker, Harry Potter, Frodo, Anne of Green Gables, Ariel, or Sleeping Beauty, they can recognize the strands of truth and deception in them. We want them to be able to recognize the great themes of the gospel: sacrificial love, the laying down of our life for our enemies, the resurrection, and lordly reign. We want them to identify forgiveness, justice, redemption, and the fight against evil, whether that comes to them from their McGuffey Reader or from Optimus Prime. Saturating our children in the one good story will enable them to discern both truth and error as it comes to them from the world.

Why Let Them See Anything At All?

Why would we want our children to be familiar with any modern media at all? Why not just tell them that they can't watch any movies or television, listen to any music less than two hundred years old, or read any modern books? Why? The gospel gives us three reasons.

First, our children will eventually grow up and become self-governing individuals. This is good and a part of the natural course of life, but because the gospel tells us that they are innately sinful, they will undoubtedly make some unwise choices. Our hope is that if we have taught them how to discern the one good story and judge every other story by it, they'll be better equipped to answer the wicked Imposter's lies when they hear them.

Second, the gospel tells us that evil does not have its origin solely from outside us. Jesus himself corrected the Pharisees' misconception about what defiles a person when he said, "What comes *out* of a person is what defiles him" (Mark 7:20). Our propensity for evil is basic and insidious to our nature. We don't need anyone to teach us how to sin, and we can't keep the evil out, because it resides within us. It comes to us from our own sinful nature, and even though we might try to protect ourselves from it, as M. Night Shyamalan's 2004 movie, *The Village*, demonstrates, you just can't keep it out. Wherever we are, evil is there—not just the potential for evil but real evil. What is already in our hearts is what defiles us, not what comes to us from media.

Finally, the gospel teaches us that God has called us to minister to our media-saturated culture. We haven't been called to minister in the 1800s or even the 1950s. Whether we like it or not, our neighbors know everything there is to know about music, TV, and movies. *It is the very language they speak; it informs and shapes all their philosophies and desires.* Yes, of course we have a different language, philosophy, and desire. We are different, but our difference should not be because we don't know who Voldemort is. We're different because we know the one good story and it has transformed our lives and freed us from the real Voldemort, and our neighbors need to know it.

Please don't misunderstand. We're not saying that every movie or even many movies are suitable for our children. But some are, and some are so iconic that at least a familiarity with them is necessary to build bridges to our neighbors. We don't want to be known as the strange family that hates everything the neighborhood likes. We want to be known as the strange family that overflows with love, service, and joy. Here are a few questions you can ask yourself as you seek to discern wisdom about exposure to media (TV, music, video games, and movies):

- Does this media outlet have any redeeming value to it? In other words, is there any way that we can use it to illustrate the one good story? Are the great themes of the gospel apparent (even though it may not be a "Christian" production)?

- Are our children unduly influenced by this movie or program? Do they mimic inappropriate words or phrases after spending time interacting with it?

- Are our children able to articulate what is lacking in this video or song? Do they see how it is contrary to the gospel? Are they able to tell you where they see the one good story in it?

- What is your child's attitude when he's denied access to this program? Has it become an idol in his heart, a god that promises him happiness?

- Is there any way that you can demonstrate a willingness to compromise with your child over this song? For instance, instead of saying no to an entire album, perhaps you could find a couple of songs on it that would be acceptable.

- Are you being ruled by fear of what might happen if your child watches or listens to this program or album? Or, are you able to think clearly about the influence the entertainment may or may not have over your child?

Remember Their Childishness

Children are called children because they are still thinking and reasoning in childish ways. They do not have the maturity to filter out words and images that overwhelm them. We have to be wise for them and judge what kinds of material they are able to process.

We know from Scripture that words can enter the heart or inner person of children and adults (Ps. 119:11; Jer. 15:16). Because of this, little children should be sheltered from images that are frightening, because they don't understand that there is a way to make an image look real on the movie screen that is not real. In their childishness, they simply believe their eyes. So when their eyes see something that is overwhelmingly scary, they'll take that image with them. Children should be protected from monsters.

Children should also be protected from images that portray boys and girls or men and women acting in ways that they are not able to understand. Little children do not need to watch kissing or any other form of sexuality, simply because they are still reasoning like children. They do not understand everything else that accompanies godly relationships. They can watch as their father and mother are affectionate (within certain limits, of course) because they know that this loving activity is carried on in the context of a loving, committed relationship. But they must be protected from any sort of illicit or prolonged sexual content.

Little girls should be protected from thinking that their worth is measured by whether a little boy likes them and thinks they're cute or pretty. They need to be taught that love has been given to them by their Savior and that they don't need to dress up like a princess to get it. They can be taught that they are the love and delight of their Savior and that he is indeed the great Prince of heaven. They can read stories about princesses and dress up and pretend. They can use their imagination to imagine being loved by a great prince because, after all, they have been.

Boys should be encouraged to love their sisters and friends who are girls and to respect women and not treat them as having no value except in their appearance. Young boys need to be taught to love, respect, and protect girls because they have been created in the image of God and have been loved by the great warrior Prince.

True Modesty

Another area that calls for real discernment is fashion—clothes, accessories, and hair styles. Whether it's little Megan's princess dresses or a teenager's bathing suit or brand-name running shoes, defining modest dress is a flashpoint in many families. In order to discover gospel truth here, we've got to define modesty in light of the one good story. Unfortunately, modesty is commonly defined in an overly simplistic way—don't wear this, do wear that—but true modesty that eventuates in modest dress is much deeper.

Here's a passage that describes the modesty of the beloved Son:

> Have this mind among yourselves, which is yours in Christ Jesus, who, though he was in the form of God, did not count equality with God a thing to be grasped, but made himself nothing, taking the form of a servant, being born in the likeness of men. And being found in human form, he humbled himself by becoming obedient to the point of death, even death on a cross. (Phil. 2:5–8)

The modesty that we see in the beloved Son's life is a refusal to show off or insist that everyone give him is due. He didn't proclaim his greatness in the streets (Matt. 12:19); he didn't show off in front of his enemy (Matt. 4:1–11). Although he could have called down legions of angels or obliterated all his detractors and the ever-so-slow disciples, he restrained himself. He didn't need our approval or praise. He had nothing to prove, and he lived humbly because he loved us and never showed off.

Our children need to be taught this kind of gospel modesty. Yes, girls should be taught to dress in an appropriate way for the simple reason that they are to walk in their Savior's footsteps. He humbled himself and served others because he loved. They should humble themselves, too, refusing to show off their body in any way because they love their Christian brothers and don't want to tempt them to lust.

But young men should be modest in their attire and demeanor, too. Just because Grandma is willing to pay for those $250 track shoes doesn't mean that Johnnie should have them. Owning so expensive a pair of shoes may tempt Johnnie to pride and his friends to envy.

Families who pride themselves on their old-fashioned apparel may need to look again at the one good story too. The only clothing that is truly holy is the robe of righteousness Jesus has given to us. He has the right to bless us in this way because he is clothed in our flesh. Our clothing with his goodness is a clothing of the heart in humility and love for our neighbor, not in outward appearances that have absolutely no value against fleshly indulgences, but rather stirs them up (Col. 2:20–23). If we are proud of the way we dress, whether fashionably or unfashionably, we're forgetting our true clothing. "Nothing gives one a more spuriously good conscience than keeping rules, even if there has been a total absence of all real charity and faith."[10] Modesty is primarily a matter of the heart and secondarily a matter of dress. Here are some questions you can ask yourself when you're faced with an apparel decision for your child:

- Do I notice a difference in the way my child acts when she wears a certain style of clothing?
- Does he act desperate when trying to get me to buy him a brand-name shirt or expensive shoes?
- Is this just a style preference? Or is there someone that my child is trying to mimic? If so, is this person someone who loves the Lord?
- Is my child willing to spend exorbitant sums of money for a new pair of jeans when there are other more important items that she needs?
- Does this piece of clothing accentuate or show off a part of my child's body in an inappropriate or attention-grabbing way? Do these clothes shout, "Look at me! See how beautiful I am!"?
- Can my child still see the joys of the gospel when she wears old clothes or doesn't get her hair cut the way she wants?
- Does my child understand that loving her Christian brothers and keeping them from temptation is the fruit of Jesus's work in her heart?

Loving the Stranger

We opened this chapter with the passage from Leviticus about loving the stranger in our neighborhood, yet here's a passage from the New Testament that seems to command isolation from the world:

> Do not love the world or the things in the world. If anyone loves the world, the love of the Father is not in him. For all that is in the world—the desires of the flesh and the desires of the eyes and pride in possessions—is not from the Father but is from the world. And the world is passing away along with its desires, but whoever does the will of God abides forever. (1 John 2:15–17)

Please notice what this verse is saying and what it isn't saying. It is saying that it is possible to have an attachment to this world's way of doing business, of acquiring possessions, that is absolutely antithetical and opposed to the love of the Father. We all are drawn by the siren's song of *Vanity Fair*. All of us are tempted to love things and take ultimate pride in our accomplishments. But this verse teaches us that if we continually maintain a strong love of the things that make us proud, make us look good, and prove our worth, then we haven't really known the "love of the Father." Why? Because the love of the Father is so glorious, so rich and beautiful, that these paltry baubles have no power to entice us, at least not for long.

Please also notice what this verse is not saying. It is not saying that we withhold love from the *people* in the world. How could the Father, who so loved the world that he sent his Son to die for it, command us not to love it? We need to be very careful here not to confuse isolation from unsaved people with true holiness. One pastor wrote these wise words to us:

> Frequently we lose sight of that fact that the gospel reaches beyond our own families. We grow content with having nice children who say "please" and "thank you," and we forget that the gospel is meant to inform all of our relationships, especially the ones we have with those outside. Remembering the truths of the gospel and that they are for *those sinners, the ones out there*, will keep the parents from seeing gospel centeredness merely as a cul-de-sac where we have pious, covenant families who live only for their own holiness rather than giving themselves and their children away for the cause of the gospel and advancement of the kingdom. Christ is on mission from his throne, by his Spirit, through the church and our family, to the world, for his glory. We join in the mission of Christ as he turns to his own and says, "as the Father

has sent me, so I send you." We are called to be the "light of the world." . . . Because of Christ's mission to seek and save the lost, we are to become part of the same narrative and see ourselves as real actors in the drama of his redemptive story.[11]

We are the real actors in this drama. Our children are real actors in this story. God has written the script, and the whole universe is his stage. The finale of this play will be the complete revelation and glorification of all that Jesus has done. He left the comfort of his home, where everything was perfectly pure, and was crucified "outside the gate" of the city (Heb. 13:12). He is ruling over all his church and over all the universe right now, imploring his people to be reconciled to him *through us, through our family!* Imagine how your neighborhood would be transformed if you loved your neighbor and encouraged your children to do that too.

Sure, this way of looking at questionable things is more difficult than simply moving to the country and living life isolated from the world. A list is always so much easier, isn't it? But if you sincerely desire to learn how to interact with your neighbors for the sake of the gospel, you'll learn to rely on the direction of the Holy Spirit. Sometimes you'll make mistakes. But you'll also incarnate your Savior to your neighbors and after all, that's the reason he has you here: "All the gifts which we possess have been bestowed by God and entrusted to us on condition that they be distributed for our neighbors' benefit."[12]

Remembering God's Grace

Please don't ignore what the Holy Spirit might be doing in your heart through this chapter. Do take the time to think deeply about it and answer the questions.

1) How can we use everyday situations to remind our children of the one good story?

2) When making decisions about interaction with the surrounding worldly culture, are you more or less protective? What is your primary motivation when making these decisions? How does reliance on the Holy Spirit help you in making decisions for your children?

3) How does Jesus's interaction with and pursuit of sinners inform the way you view social situations with unbelievers? When would you need to disallow association with an unbeliever?

4) Why is it important to let our children interface with society and its varied forms of entertainment?

5) How would you define modesty? How can you help your children understand the importance of modesty?

6) How does your family fit into the one good story?

7) Summarize in three or four sentences what you have learned in this chapter.

8

Go and Tell Your Father

The knowledge of God's Father-love is the first and simplest, but also the last and highest lesson in the school of prayer.

~ **ANDREW MURRAY**[1]

Practically everyone has an "Aunt Biddy" sort of person in his life. You know, she's the relative your parents had to tell you to be nice to. She's also the one who has the inheritance, so you know it's to your advantage to be nice and visit her, but it's just so hard. It's hard because you know that she doesn't really approve of you. She always sniffs when you come in, and you know that she'll tell your mother about all your miscues after you leave. Even though you know she has the resources to help you out when you get into a jam, you're loathe to ask her because she'll sniff at you even more and make you grovel a little and explain why it is that you need her help—again.

Conversely, when my grandkids come over on family night, they run into the house and hug me, and every one of them wants to talk to me at the same time. I have to shoo them out of the kitchen while I'm making dinner because they want to watch and help and jabber. They each have a story to share, and frequently I have to listen to two or three of them at once. I'm Mimi. I'm not Aunt Biddy!

The difference between the relationship we have with our personal "Aunt Biddy" and the relationship my grandchildren have with their Mimi can be summed up in one word, love. These little darlings know that I love them and that I am delighted when they walk through the door. Love makes all the difference in their comfort level with me. I don't sniff at them, I draw them close and snuggle them. They are assured of my love, so they run toward me and jump on my lap and tell jokes and stories and ask for candy. They share their sorrows. They know I'll listen. They're comfortable with me and love me because they know that I love them.

Praying to Aunt Biddy

When it comes to prayer, most of us simply feel guilty. We know we should pray, we know that we should present our requests to God, but for most of us (and for our kids), if we're honest, we'll admit that praying to God is a little like visiting with cranky old Aunt Biddy. Of course, theologically we know that's not the truth; we know that "God is love" (1 John 4:8), but at heart we're not really sure that our prayer amounts to anything more than lifeless protocol demanded by a disappointed father who sniffs at us, disapproves, and exacts some sort of obeisance before he opens up the bank vault to pinch out a little trinket from his treasures. Run into his presence? Raid the fridge? Do our laundry? Ask for candy? From God? Hardly. How could we possibly think about him in that way? After all, he isn't our Mimi. He's the holy God, Lord of heaven and earth, who understands every thought and intention in our hearts. "And no creature is hidden from his sight, but all are naked and exposed to the eyes of him to whom we must give account" (Heb. 4:13). Have an open and loving conversation with him? How?

You'll remember that in chapter 5 we introduced to you this acrostic: MNTCP (Moms Need To Constantly Pray). At that time you may have been struggling to remember that each of those letters also stood for Manage, Nurture, Train, Correct, and Promise. You probably gave some sort of mental assent to the need for prayer (for both moms and dads) and then moved on to the more "practical" side of the message: learning when to manage, when to train, how to remind your kids of God's promises. You might have thought, Yes, of course, parents need to constantly pray. Yes, of course. Next?

In this chapter we are going to encourage you to take another look at the role of prayer in parenting, but before we get started, we want to remind you of one thing: your child's salvation does not depend on your faithfulness in prayer. It depends solely on the prayer of your faithful High Priest,

Jesus Christ. Yes, he does use means, and yes, he does answer prayer, but your prayers are not the lynchpin upon which everything depends. Salvation is of the Lord.

Every Christian knows that we have been commanded to pray, but our prayer life is frequently cold and lifeless. It tends to be just another chore on our daily checklist. Most of us don't have the same enthusiasm about it that we have if we are going for a visit to a beloved friend's house whose generosity always dazzles us. Our time in prayer is frequently more like a visit to Aunt Biddy's. We tend to be lazy about it because we're not thrilled about spending time with God. Very often we discover that our plan to pray once we get the kids going on their math is thwarted—again. Could it be that our aversion to prayer is because we are trying to motivate ourselves to pray through guilt? Guilt will never eventuate in sincere prayer. Guilt never motivates us to do anything wildly loving.

Praying to Your Loving Father

As Andrew Murray writes:

> This is the one chief thought on which Jesus dwells. He would have us see that the secret of effectual prayer is *to have the heart filled with the father love of God*. It is not enough for us to know that God is a father; he would have us come under the full impression of what that name implies. We must take the best earthly father we know; we must think of the tenderness and love with which he regards the request of his child, the love and joy with which he grants every reasonable desire. We must then, as we think in adoring worship of the infinite love and fatherliness of God, consider how with much more tenderness and joy he sees us come to him and gives us what we ask aright. And then, when we see how much this divine arithmetic is beyond our comprehension and feel how impossible it is for us to apprehend God's readiness to hear us, he would have us come and open our heart for the Holy Spirit to shed abroad God's father love there.[2]

What you need as a praying parent is a deep drink of the great love of God, your Father, not more commands to pray. You know you should pray about your parenting. Do you know how he loves you? Apprehending his love for you will change your prayer time from visits with Aunt Biddy to family dinners with Mimi. The Lord isn't disappointed in you or in your parenting.

He's not disappointed in your prayers. He doesn't treat his dear children as "disappointments" whose disobedience and failures take him by surprise or shock him. He does not suspend his love until they get their acts back together. He already knows the worst about you (in yourself) and loves and approves you nonetheless (in Christ). Although your sin does grieve him (Eph. 4:30), he doesn't want you to keep your distance, sitting in a corner wearing a dunce cap until you learn your lessons. He invites you to come boldly in with joy and confidence, knowing that he is eager to embrace you. You, as a sinner who trusts his Son, Jesus, are able to do that because the Son prays and intercedes for you. The Father loves you. Take a few moments to meditate on the verses below and ask the Spirit to give you faith to believe that Jesus's prayer and entreaty are powerful enough to change you from an enemy to a beloved child. Because of Jesus, your Father delights to hear the sound of your voice, the same way I love to hear my grandchild's voice, except exponentially more so.

> [Jesus] poured out his soul to death and was numbered with the transgressors [that's us!]; yet he bore the sin of many, and makes intercession for the transgressors. (Isa. 53:12)

> Consequently, he is able to save to the uttermost those who *draw near to God* through him, since he *always lives to make intercession* for them. (Heb. 7:25)

> For Christ has entered, not into holy places made with hands, which are copies of the true things, but into heaven itself, now to appear in the presence of God *on our behalf.* (Heb. 9:24)

> For there is one God, and there is one mediator [intercessor] between God and men, *the man Christ Jesus, who gave himself as a ransom for all.* (1 Tim. 2:5–6)

> My little children, I am writing these things to you so that you may not sin. But if anyone does sin, *we have an advocate [intercessor] with the Father*, Jesus Christ the righteous. (1 John 2:1)

Have you ever had the experience of gaining admittance to a private event because you were with someone who had an in? I have. It's nice to walk up to the stern guard at the door and say, "I'm with him," and then watch the guard's face soften into welcome as he opens the door wide. Here's the truth: when you walk into the throne-room of the holy King of the universe, Jesus is standing by your side. You can simply say, "I'm with him," and all of heaven is at your disposal. When we forget who we are with and who is interceding for us, we start to think that we have to get our act together before God would be interested in hearing from us. When that happens, we do all sorts of foolish things, like boast about who is the greatest. Here's how Paul speaks peace to our hearts: "So let no one boast in men. For all things are yours, whether Paul or Apollos or Cephas or the world or life or death or the present or the future—all are yours, and you are Christ's, and Christ is God's" (1 Cor. 3:21–23).

All things are ours! Every answer to prayer that we need is ours. When we soak our soul in the grace of the gospel, we'll find our desire to spend time with him in prayer changing. We'll be more comfortable in our set times of prayer, and we'll also begin to carry on a nonstop conversation with him in our heart because we know that he loves to hear our voice. Then, when we are faced with a difficult decision, or when the kids are fighting or need correction, we will be comfortable running to him. "Lord, I know you're here. Help me see you. Give me grace"—that will be our heart's frequent cry. Because the Holy Spirit loves to make Jesus grand in our eyes, he'll nurture, train, and remind us of his gracious condescension. And when we forget the gospel, he'll gently correct us and make Jesus appear grand to us again. Are the kids making you a little crazy today? Remember, you can pray, "I know I'm with you, Lord, and you have given everything to me. Please help me see you now."

You can also have confidence when you pray because your heavenly Father loves you—yes, you, personally. He loves you because you are in the Son he loves; yes, but also because he has chosen to set his love upon you. Why? I don't know. When my grandchildren ask me why I love them, I don't get out my list of all the things they do that make them worthy of my love. If they ask me why I love them, I simply say, "Because you're you and I love you." In a way, that's how it is with your heavenly Father; but he has been loving you since before there was a you to love. Actually, from the foundation of the world he predestined us in love (Eph. 1:4–5). He was able to look down through all the corridors of time and see you and say, "I love him, I love her." Here's how the apostle John wrote about God's incomprehensible love for us:

In that day you will ask in my name, and I do not say to you that I will ask the Father on your behalf; *for the Father himself loves you*, because you have loved me and have believed that I came from God. (John 16:26–27)

I do not ask for these only, but also for those who will believe in me through their word. . . . I in them and you in me, that they may become perfectly one, so that the world may know that you sent me and *loved them even as you loved me.* (John 17:20, 23)

See what kind of love the Father has given to us, that we should be called children of God; and so we are. (1 John 3:1)

No wonder Paul prayed that we might be given the ability to comprehend the incomprehensible: God's love for us in Christ. We'll never get to the end of this. We'll never plumb the depths of his love; even in eternity we'll be surprised by grace every day. Paul prayed that we "may have strength to comprehend with all the saints what is the breadth and length and height and depth, and to know the love of Christ that surpasses knowledge" (Eph. 3:18–19). In light of all our unbelief, it really does take the strength of God to believe this: God loves us. When we begin to grow in this confidence, a confidence that comes from grace, not from our own works, we'll grow in our desire to pray too. He isn't Aunt Biddy. He's our loving Father. Here are precious words again from Andrew Murray:

In all the compassion with which a father listens to his weak or sickly child, in all the joy with which he hears his stammering child, in all the gentle patience with which he bears with a thoughtless child, we must, as in so many mirrors, *study the heart of our God's readiness to hear us*, then He would have us come and open our heart for the Holy Spirit to shed abroad God's Father-love there.[3]

Desperation Creates Praying Parents

Aside from questioning whether our Father really loves us and wants to hear our prayer, another reason we don't pray is that we are not really desperate. If we've been lulled into complacency and self-reliance because we have compliant children today, we probably won't feel much of a need to pray. As Paul Miller, author of *A Praying Life*, admits:

It took me seventeen years to realize I couldn't parent on my own. It was not a great spiritual insight, just a realistic observation. If I didn't pray deliberately and reflectively for members of my family by name every morning, they'd kill each other. I was incapable of getting inside their hearts. I was desperate. But even more, I couldn't change my self-confident heart . . . [I came to realize that] I did my best parenting by prayer. I began to speak less to the kids and more to God. It was actually quite relaxing.[4]

The Lord is kind to us to make us desperate for him, but when we feel desperate we frequently don't pray. Instead we get out our books and try to figure out what we're doing wrong rather than falling on our knees and pleading with our Father for grace. We double-down our efforts to get the kids to do our bidding, and we feel as though we don't have time for prayer.

We know that being a busy mom or dad frequently does make us feel as though we just don't have time to pray. *Pray? I can barely breathe!* Even if that's the case, if you ask for grace, the Lord will enable you to carry on a nonstop conversation with him in your heart all day long. *Lord, please grant us mercy now. Lord, I need your grace to respond to their bickering with gentleness now. Lord, please give me wisdom to see the cross in this.* This sort of unspoken prayer will help you begin to rely more on him than on yourself.

Now, Pray Like Missionaries

The remembrance of Christ's intercession, our Father's love for us, and our desperation are the fuel that we need to build the fire of fervent prayer in our hearts. Guilt won't do it. Laws about it will only crush us or make us self-righteous like the Pharisee in Luke 18. What we need is grace. And we need his grace in our parenting too. We need grace to see him everywhere, grace to lavish on our children. So, as we talk to you now about how to pray for your parenting and how to pray for your children, please don't forget everything we've just said. Remember, we "only maintain that our confidence cannot rest on anything else than the mercy of God alone."[5]

All Christian parents are missionaries. We are all on a mission from the Lord to announce the love of the Father to our children and to encourage them, as much as we can, to believe it. We're to tell them of the law so that they know that they need rescue, and then we're to tell them of the Rescuer who has freed them from the law's curse. But this monumental task is utterly impossible for us to accomplish on our own. We need rescue; we need a

Rescuer too. So we need to pray for help. What follows are some examples of the prayers that another missionary, Paul, prayed. They will enlighten and direct our prayer away from the kinds of prayer that we're tempted as parents to pray—Lord, just make them behave!—to those that more clearly reflect our mission as Christ's representatives.

Paul's prayers to the different churches have similar patterns. As we explore these patterns, we can learn how to pray for our personal mission field.

I (Jessica) have learned that the first section of Paul's prayers is always filled with thankfulness for the people to whom he was speaking. In fact, he simply gushes with thanksgiving, speaking of his love for those people in astounding terms. Listen to the warm language he uses with his family in Philippi: "I yearn for you all with the affection of Christ Jesus" (Phil. 1:8). Paul longed to see the Thessalonians and wondered, "What thanksgiving can we return to God for you?" (1 Thess. 3:9). To the Romans he was filled with thanks and longing to be with them (Rom. 1:8, 11). He told the Ephesians that he did not cease to give thanks for them, remembering them in his prayers (Eph. 1:16).

Paul never shied away from praying with fervent fondness for his children in Christ. In the same way, our prayers for our children should overflow with thanksgiving. Of course, Paul didn't have to wake up at 3:00 AM to feed a screaming baby, to break up the fourteenth fight of the day, or to bear the cruel remarks of an angry teenager. I know that Paul didn't have to do those things, but he loved all those churches as if they were his children. He did have to rebuke them and bear with them as they sinned against him and each other. These weren't model churches with perfect congregations; they were churches made up of God's children, sinners in need of grace. Paul was trying to see them the way Christ saw them and trying to love them the way he had been loved.

In the same way, we can ask the Holy Spirit to help us see our children like he does, with great hope and love. We can ask him to help us be "grace detectives," to be more aware of how the Lord is working in their life than in how they are failing. I'm trying to learn to start each of my prayers for my kids with words something like this: *Lord, I thank you for Johnnie. Please help me see where you're working in him. Thank you that you've sustained his life. Thank you that he's not pretending to be a believer. Thank you that he's still in our home.*

After Paul's time of thanksgiving for the people, he goes on to tell them of his prayer for them. He prays for them the same sort of Christian-living prayers we typically pray. He prays that they would walk worthy of their calling, do good, and be filled with knowledge and wisdom. He prays that the Lord would give them grace to love each other more and that they would be restored to perfect fellowship with the Lord and with one another. These are the types of prayers I previously offered for our children. I was focused solely on their behavior. *Lord, please help Josh to be kind today and have self-control.* We can pray for our children's salvation or for their future spouse, but typically I limited my prayers to the behaviors that affected me most.

After these first two steps, Paul's prayers differ from the way I normally pray. He does pray that they would love one another, but always in light of the way they have been loved. He prays that they would have knowledge and insight, but always a knowledge and insight about Christ's love for them. He prays that they would know Jesus's power at work in them. Yes, he does pray that they would do good but not so that he would look good or because he has worked so hard for them. He prays that they would respond in gratitude for Jesus Christ. He asks the Lord to help them become pure and blameless but only in light of the fact that they are already called pure and blameless by God.

If we have unregenerate children, we should be fervently calling out to God, pleading that they would see the riches and fullness of Christ's grace. In fact, praying that every member of the family would believe in his grace should be our constant prayer. Our prayers should echo Paul's, prayers asking that our children's eyes would be open to the glorious power of God that created the heavens and yet intimately cares for their souls.

Paul exuded confidence in every prayer in God's work in the churches. When we listen, we can hear him praying and believing that his prayers had already born fruit. This confidence didn't come from his trust in his fellow saints; he was very well acquainted with their failures. Instead his confidence came from God. He knew that by the faithful Lord's power, the Lord would establish and guard them. He prayed that each one would be "strengthened with power through his Spirit" (Eph. 3:16), because "he who calls you is faithful; he will surely do it" (1 Thess. 5:24). Paul was confident in his prayers, because he believed Christ's words on the cross. When Jesus uttered those three glorious words, "It is finished" (John 19:30), it meant that "he who began a good work in you will bring it to completion" (Phil. 1:6).

I (Jessica) admit that at times my prayer for my children is nothing more than vocalized unbelief aimed at God. Imagine that my son has been angry and unkind, hurting me and others for the past two hours. When he finally comes to me and asks for prayer, I can barely muster, "Lord, help him to stop crying and be nice." I pray that way because I am angry and because I have forgotten who is at work here. I don't believe that anything more than feigned repentance is happening. I doubt that he'll ever change. So, when he asks me to pray, I do, but I don't have any thanksgiving or faith to see what the Lord is up to. I'm forgetting that it is not my feeble attempts at parenting that are going to change this child. I forget that it is God at work in him.

Sometimes the Holy Spirit reminds me that I can pray with confidence that he will be changed, not because of my great prayer or parenting but because this is what God is working toward also. But in those moments of anger, I feel alone and helpless in my parenting. I feel utterly confused and weak in my parenting. But the truth is I am not alone, I have the Helper, and he is teaching me that I must have confidence in his strength, not my own.

So, by faith I'm learning to rephrase my prayer. Instead of praying that our son would stop crying and be nice, I begin to thank God for him. I thank God that our son has been entrusted to our family. I thank God that our son has come to me for help and that he is beginning to believe that prayer can make a difference. I do pray that the Lord would help him love his siblings, and then I begin to remind both of us of what Jesus has already done for us. Jesus lived in a family with irritating siblings. They certainly were selfish and sinned against him, yet he loved them. I remind myself and my dear son in prayer that this matters because, if he would believe it, this record of love can be his too. The Lord has beautifully transformed my heart. Instead of being focused on all that I am suffering, I am able to remember his sufferings and look to him for grace.

Parents can pray for their children with thanksgiving, purpose, and confidence. We can pray this way for ourselves also. In moments of weakness and desperation, when our children seem to have forgotten everything we've ever said, we can begin our communication with our Father by praying that we would see what he has already done for us. We can be thankful for God's work in our children and in us. Once our hearts are settled in his great love for us, we can pray that he would open our eyes so that we can see how magnificent he is. He has loved us and called us his dear children. Because of his loving welcome, we can love our children, and they can learn to love too. Then, remembering that he is "able to do far more abundantly than all that we ask or think, according to the power at work within us" (Eph. 3:20) will boost our faith to pray prayers that are simply mind-boggling. Can the Lord really save *that* child? Is he able to teach *her* about his love? Will they ever really come to know and believe it?

He Always Hears His Son's Prayer

"Since then we have a great high priest who has passed through the heavens, Jesus, the Son of God, let us hold fast our confession. For we do not have a high priest who is unable to sympathize with our weaknesses, but one who in every respect has been tempted as we are, yet without sin. Let us then with confidence draw near to the throne of grace, that we may receive mercy and find grace to help in time of need" (Heb. 4:14–16). Jesus Christ has blazed a trail into heaven for us. He did this by sacrificing his blood, allowing his flesh to be torn so that the pathway into the Father's presence would forever be open to us. He has annihilated every obstacle that would bar our entrance into the Most Holy Place, where our prayer-answering Father dwells. From his first breath he lived a life of perfect dependence on his Father, carrying on a continual conversation with him, giving thanks, submitting himself. Jesus Christ always prayed without ceasing and always in accordance with his Father's will. He shed tears and voiced loud cries all the days of his flesh so that his prayer life would be completely righteous, one of perfect reliance and submission. He did this because he loved conversing with his Father but also so that our record before our Father would be one of perfect prayer and submission too.

We don't need to try to pray to prove that we're properly pious or really serious. Instead we pray because we are completely assured that the Father hears our prayers *because they come to him through the lips of his dear Son.*

Are your prayers weak, scrambled, inconsistent, self-centered? Of course they are. If we think they are anything else, we are very close to sliding into the self-righteous prayer that Jesus warned against in Luke 18. Even so, we can take heart because the true cries of our heart are always voiced by the beloved Son, our great High Priest.

So, lean into him. Don't be afraid that you'll fail at this. Don't think he'll judge you because you don't say the right words with the right inflection and all the proper theology. Don't think that he'll sniff at your requests because your family is such a mess. Be assured that these things will never happen, for one simple reason: the record of our prayer has already been written. The Father hears the perfectly worded, properly believing, and flawlessly theologically correct prayers of his beloved Son when you pray.

We can freely pour out our heart to our Father knowing that our dear Savior will purify and transform our words into petitions that please him. When your prayer is freely spoken, joyful, and honest, your children will learn to pray that way too. Teach them that he is the high King of heaven, yes, a person not to be trifled with. But also teach them that he is their dear Father, one who delights to hear their requests, even when they say them all wrong and don't have much faith and mumble them as a last resort. Go tell your Father about everything that's in your heart, and don't be afraid. The Lord Jesus is mediating for us all.

Remembering God's Grace

Please don't ignore what the Holy Spirit might be doing in your heart through this chapter. Please do take the time to think deeply about it and answer the questions.

1) Does your opinion of God the Father invite or discourage you in prayer? Do you think God is disappointed with you?
2) Have you hesitated to pray because you have believed that your standing before God has something to do with your good works, especially concerning how well you are doing as a parent?
3) How does believing the gospel change the way you think about prayer?

4) Do Paul's prayers for the churches help you to see how your prayers for your children could be different? In what ways?

5) How does the fact that the Son prays perfectly on your behalf encourage you in your prayer life?

6) Summarize in three or four sentences what you have learned in this chapter.

9

Weak Parents and Their Strong Savior

I thought parenting was going to portray my strengths, never realizing
that God had ordained it to reveal my weaknesses.
~ **DAVE HARVEY**[1]

"I hate you, and I'm never coming back!" The door slammed and Aaron was gone. His dad and mom broke down into tears—again. All they wanted was for Aaron to realize how much they loved him and wanted what was best for him. But all Aaron could see was how controlling and strict his parents were compared to every other parent he knew. Both Aaron and his parents felt misunderstood, hurt, and angry. Aaron had threatened so many times to leave, but his parents never really thought he would. How would they explain this to their church? Their family had long been lauded as the exemplary shining star of the church. All their kids had been so well-behaved, polite, and kind. Bob and Karen had been told so many times by so many people that they were great parents, they had started to make it their identity. But in the last year their youngest had decided it was time to rebel against everything they had ever taught him. They were totally befuddled by this. They had raised each of their children in exactly the same way. Why did the others turn out so well, and why did Aaron hate them so much?

"Lord, where are you? We thought you would bless our efforts. We've done everything we could do. We thought you would turn his heart toward you. Why is this happening? Where did we go wrong?"

~

Locked in the bathroom, Shelley couldn't believe what was happening. She could hear her kids screaming in the other room. Her twin boys were at it again, fighting over some toy they had played with a gazillion times. Why couldn't they just take turns? What happened to the timer she had bought them so they wouldn't have this problem? She wanted to go into the living room, take all their toys, and throw them in the trash. But their fighting wasn't even what was troubling her the most at the moment. She had just found a stash of e-mails on her computer that were between a sixteen-year-old boy at church and her fourteen-year-old daughter. How could she have been so blind? She had no idea that her daughter even had a boyfriend or an e-mail account. The e-mails started out innocent enough but had grown into something she was embarrassed and angered to read. Not only had her daughter been lying to her, but she had been stealing from her in order to buy little gifts for this boy. Shelley knew the boy from church, and he was not the type she would ever want her daughter to talk to, let alone be "in love" with. The pain in the pit of her stomach kept getting stronger and stronger as she recalled the words that were emblazoned on the screen. Emily and Dave were supposed to meet today to "show each other how much they loved each other."

She wished she could go to her husband for help, but he was out of town, again. He wouldn't be home for two more days. And even when he was home, he never seemed as concerned as she was about the kids' behavior anyway. His typical response was, "They're kids; kids will be kids." Shelley sat on the floor, crying into a towel. When did her life take this horrible turn? She had been faithful to go to church. She had worked full-time just so her kids could go to a Christian school. She wanted to protect her daughter from the very situation that had gotten Shelley herself pregnant and married by the time she was nineteen.

Shelley had prayed for her kids almost daily. She had been the leader of the Mom's-In-Touch group at their school until last year when she had to quit going to the prayer meetings because the pressures of working, driving to piano and baseball practice and games, cleaning the house, and making dinner had just been too much for her. Was this God's way of punishing her?

Should she have been more involved in their youth group, more involved in their school?

Parenting for the Glory of God

In the mid-1600s godly men gathered together in London, England, for the express purpose of developing a teaching tool for training believers in the faith. The first question they asked and answered was, "What is the chief end of man?" In modern jargon we might ask, "What's the deal? Why are we here?" Their answer to this question of ultimate meaning has survived for centuries: "Man's chief end is to glorify God, and to enjoy him forever." The definitive reason for our existence is to glorify God with our lives and to enjoy him now and forever, throughout all eternity. Very simply, for us to glorify God means that we recognize God's majesty in all things and make him appear as glorious as he already is through our words and lives.

Every true Christian sincerely desires to glorify God in this way by worship and obedience. We all hope to one day hear those blessed words, "Well done, good and faithful servant" (Matt. 25:21). All godly parents also earnestly hope that their children will glorify the Lord. We want our children to be useful and faithful servants who will one day hear that "good and faithful" benediction too. And although it is right and good that we desire these things, the truth is that none of us knows how God has ordained that we would glorify him. The Lord uses each of his unique children in unique ways. Perhaps the way that he's chosen for us to make much of him is through intense familial suffering. Perhaps it will be through sin and failure, maybe even through untimely death (John 21:19).

Yes, every believer is called to consciously seek to glorify him, but we're not the only ones who do. God is too great to be glorified only through the lives of his victorious children. He is glorified by our suffering and even by our sin. His sustaining strength is glorified when we walk through the furnace of affliction. His mercy and patience are glorified when he continues to love us despite our failures. He is so great that he is even glorified by the evil in the world. Paul put it this way: "For from him and through him and to him are all things. To him be glory forever" (Rom. 11:36).[2]

> Everything comes from him;
> Everything happens through him;
> Everything ends up in him.
> Always glory! Always praise! (Rom. 11:36 MESSAGE)

Everything that happens does so for only one reason—*to glorify God*. God reigns as the majesty on high, ruler over all, using pagan kings as his servants to exalt his name. Even pompous King Nebuchadnezzar's insanity resulted in the praise of God's glory:

> I blessed the Most High, and praised and honored him who lives forever,
>> for his dominion is an everlasting dominion,
>>> and his kingdom endures from generation to generation;
>> all the inhabitants of the earth are accounted as nothing,
>>> and he does according to his will among the host of heaven
>>> and among the inhabitants of the earth;
>> and none can stay his hand
>> or say to him, "What have you done?" (Dan. 4:34–35)

The Lord Jesus rules preeminently over everything, including our families, "for by [Jesus] all things were created, in heaven and on earth, visible and invisible, whether thrones or dominions or rulers or authorities—all things were created through him and for him. And he is before all things, and in him all things hold together. . . . That in everything he might be preeminent." (Col. 1:16–18)

The Lord God rules in Trinitarian sovereignty over all there is, freely ruling and overruling for his glory according to his will. As his children we long to make his glory known by our faithful obedience. That is a good desire, but a strong, successful family may not be the way he has chosen for us to glorify him. Perhaps his goal is that we glorify him by demonstrating weakness and even failure.

The Strange Ways of God

We know that this is probably a very strange concept to you. Americans generally can't wrap their minds around a success that seems like a failure. God's glory and our sins seem mutually exclusive. We treasure strength, not weakness; victory, not defeat; happy endings, not tragedies. But is this the message of the Bible? When we look closely at the Scripture, do we see people who were always faithful, always strong and victorious, people whose lives were shining examples of virtue and faithfulness? Do we see heroes who left exemplary examples for us to follow? Or do we see something else in their lives?

And then we come to the paradigm-shattering, unfathomable gospel message. Here we see a little unwed pregnant girl, a midnight flight into Egypt, an itinerate preacher from a nowhere city who attracted a crowd of nobodies for a while and ended up deserted, shamed, and hanging exposed and bloody. In the end he was confounded by his Father's absence and seemed to die in utter humiliation and defeat. How on earth can a story like that possibly ever bring the Creator of heaven and earth glory? Evil appears to have triumphed. Sin has been victorious. All is lost. God's glory might have been seen if he had been able to get everyone to hail Christ as the beloved Son worthy of all praise and obedience. But this story? This weakness? How would his glory be seen now? Had sin really triumphed over God's desire to be glorified? *God's methods turn everything we assume about his glory upside down.*

> Our fall afforded him the opportunity of showing that in the destruction of sin He could not only manifest His justice, but also glorify His mercy in remitting and forgiving sin, without infringing upon His righteousness. . . . Such is the edifice which the Almighty reared upon the ruins of sin.[3]

Our fall afforded him the opportunity of glorifying himself. In one monumental act of shocking grace, God demonstrated that he is mighty enough to transform what masquerades as utter defeat into great, God-glorifying victory. What an edifice he has "reared upon the ruins of sin"! He uses our sin and failure to magnify his mercy, justice, and wisdom. And, make no mistake about it, the sin of Judas, Peter, Caiaphas, Pontius Pilate, the blood-thirsty guards, and the mindless masses was his instrument to glorify himself in a greater measure than he had ever before been glorified. "For truly in this city there were gathered together against your holy servant Jesus, whom you anointed, both Herod and Pontius Pilate, along with the Gentiles and the peoples of Israel, *to do whatever your hand and your plan had predestined to take place* (Acts 4:27–28).

Because the Lord *always* acts for his glory, and because he had predestined the sin of the Romans and the Jews in his Son's cruel execution, their sin glorified him. It was the means he used to demonstrate his grace, mercy, justice, and love so that we would sing his praises throughout eternity. Think about this: we would never have known what mercy is if we had never sinned.

Now, before you throw this book across the room and accuse us of encouraging people to sin, please let us make a few things clear. We're not encouraging anyone to sin. God hates sin. We should hate it too. And because we never know what God's will is before it is accomplished, we must *always* assume that it is his will to be glorified by our obedience rather than by our disobedience. We must continually strive *with all our might* for the "holiness without which no one will see the Lord" (Heb. 12:14).

Further, just because God uses our failures for his glory doesn't negate the fact that, if we are saved, Jesus had to suffer God's wrath for them. Sin is serious. It caused the Son to suffer. We're not telling you to sin. We're telling you to strive against sin. We're telling you to teach your children to strive against sin. But when the inevitable happens, when you and your children do sin, when you fail miserably, you need to know that God glorifies himself in your sin. Everything God does is for his glory, and he is completely sovereign over everything that occurs. He uses our sin and the sin of our children to glorify himself. If he did not, we would not sin.[4]

Nearly every parenting book you'll read will tell you how to be a successful parent of successful, seemingly sinless children. Our modern worship of personal success stories is clearly seen in the number of books that outline the methods for producing spiritual giants. Whether they encourage family-integrated education and worship, public schools, immersing our family in the culture, or moving to a little house on the prairie, being a successful parent and raising successful kids is the only paradigm we seem to be willing to accept. But what if we're measuring success in the wrong way? Could it be that our perception of success isn't God's plan for us or for our family? What if he's going to use our failure and our children's rebellion to make us humble comforters of other sufferers for his glory?

What if he has called us to Jeremiah's ministry rather than to Daniel's? *Is there room in your parenting paradigm for weakness and failure if weakness and failure glorify God?* These are difficult questions. As we consider our own children, it is our dearest prayer that they would seek to glorify him through genuine obedience and faith. Our hearts will break and we will weep if they do not. But don't we have to be willing to say that the chief end of our parenting is not our own glorification as great parents but rather that we glorify God and enjoy him forever, *whatever* that means?

Boasting in Weakness[5]

Not unlike most other Bible characters, Paul's story isn't one of great worldly success. He would never have made the cover of *People* magazine. In his sufferings and failures, Paul was taught the value of weakness by the Lord himself. For instance, at Damascus it was the Lord's will that he sneak out of the city, in a basket under the cover of night, like a criminal. The great apostle Paul was a fugitive from justice who had to make himself very small and very quiet in order to escape persecution.

When Paul lists his ministry credentials, they don't include what we would call his "accomplishments." No, instead he boasts about his weakness in things such as afflictions, hardships, calamities, beatings, imprisonments, riots, labors, sleepless nights, and hunger (2 Cor. 6:4–5). Have you ever wondered if there was something lacking in Paul's interpersonal communication skills? Maybe he wasn't trying hard enough to get along with people; maybe he needed a book on how to have his best life now. Why would he have so much trouble if he was really serving the Lord?

Paul brags that he has the true marks of an apostle because he has had "far greater labors, far more imprisonments, with countless beatings, and [was] often near death" (2 Cor. 11:23). He was in constant "danger from rivers, danger from robbers, danger from my own people, danger from Gentiles, danger in the city, danger in the wilderness, danger at sea, danger from false brothers; in toil and hardship, through many a sleepless night, in hunger and thirst, often without food, in cold and exposure. And, apart from other things, there is the daily pressure on me of my anxiety for all the churches" (2 Cor. 11:26–28).

What would we say to a parent who had this degree of trouble in her parenting? Would we tell her that she needed to get her parenting act together? Would we parade our children or our favorite parenting method before her? Would we assure her that God wants her to overcome all her weakness so everything will run more smoothly? Paul was weak and subject to trials, just like us. *The obvious difference between Paul and us is that Paul bragged about his weakness, and we try to hide it.* We militate against it. We think that Teflon-coated, spick-and-span, seamless parenting, producing perfect little children all lined up like the Von Trapp family singers, is the only thing that can possibly glorify God. *We're making him too small and our desires too big.*

At another time, after receiving a surpassingly great revelation from God, Paul was given a thorn in his flesh to keep him from becoming conceited about what he had seen. Imagine this: here is the great apostle who had immense spiritual gifts, who prayed prayers that serve as a model for us today, yet, the Lord refused to grant his dear child's request to remove the thorn. Think again: the Lord refused to remove that thorn even though Paul prayed for its removal three times. Although we don't know what the thorn was, we do know that it was substantial. It's obvious from the passages above that Paul was familiar with real suffering, but this thorn was far worse. This thorn was ordained by God to keep Paul *humble, dependent, and weak.*

Paul also recognized that this thorn was a messenger of Satan. Here's the astonishing truth: God used Satan to keep Paul from the sin of pride. God always employs Satan to God's end, to serve God's people. God uses Satan to produce godliness in us too, just as he did in Paul. Yes, we are to resist the onslaught of our enemy, and we are to pray that the Lord protects us from Satan's attacks on our family, but these attacks may be the very tool that God uses in our lives to keep us from other sins such as pride and self-reliance.

Your continual struggles as a parent, your child's rebellion and hatred, are simply thorns in your Father's employ to keep you close to him. No one wants a thorn, especially if that thorn takes the shape of a beloved child. None of us wants to appear weak or incompetent, especially when it comes to difficulties in our family. We hate it when we can't boast about our successful parenting, yet we can grow in our faith to believe that the Lord is sending a particular trial because it glorifies him. Has the Lord granted us the privilege of choosing how we'll glorify him? Would our chosen path *ever* lead us to the valley of the shadow of death with our children? If we spend our whole life trying to avoid that valley, how will we ever experience his comfort while he sustains us by his grace *in* the valley? The thorn became the place where Paul, the apostle who wrote more on grace than anyone else, needed grace.

The weaknesses, failures, and sins of our family are the places where we learn that we need grace too. It is there, in those dark mercies, that God teaches us to be humbly dependent. It is there that he draws near to us and sweetly reveals his grace. Paul's suffering teaches us to reinterpret our thorn. Instead of seeing it as a curse, we are to see it as the very thing that keeps us "pinned close to the Lord."[6]

All-Sufficient Grace

Here are more precious words from Paul, our suffering brother, after he had been denied his prayer request to be freed from his humiliating thorn: "But [the Lord] said to me, 'My grace is sufficient for you, for my power is made perfect in weakness.' Therefore I will boast all the more gladly of my weaknesses, so that the power of Christ may rest upon me" (2 Cor. 12:9).

Paul understood that personal success and strength were *barriers* to his experience of God's grace. God's sustaining power is seen and developed in our weakness and failure. It is *never* developed anywhere else. The power of Christ flows through parents who boast in and embrace their personal weakness, not on those who think they don't need it. Of course, every one of us will quickly confess that we know we need the power of Christ. Yes, yes, of course we do. But the veracity of our confident confession will be tested in our response to our weakness and failure and to the weakness, failure, and sin of our children. Do we see these trials as God's gift to us? Do we see our children's struggles as our Savior approaching us in love to make his grace strong in our lives? Do we believe that we must have this kind of humiliation so that Christ's grace will flow through us to our family? Do we want his grace that much? Do we *really* want to glorify him?

Whether or not we like it, whether or not we understand it, it is kind of the Lord to demolish our confidence in our own strength, abilities, and cherished methods. True, it doesn't feel kind at the time. It's terribly painful to watch your beloved son turn from the faith or to hear that your daughter has been disruptive in Sunday school again. It crushes our hearts when we try and try to explain the gospel to our little ones and they stare back at us in boredom and resentment. Yet, it is a kindness when he strips us of self-reliance, because it is there, in our emptiness and brokenness, that we experience the privilege of his sustaining grace. It is only when we arrive at that dreaded place of weakness that we discover the surpassing power of Christ. It is only when we are finally freed from those oh-so-constricting straightjackets of self-righteousness that we are able to experience the true comfort and warmth of the robes of his righteousness.

His Power, Your Weakness

Our weakness is the place where we learn to depend on his power. When we're stripped of everything that we thought we could trust in, when we're absolutely desperate for help, the Lord moves into our circumstance and demonstrates his power. Sometimes he shows us his power by changing the circumstance, miraculously accomplishing what we could never accomplish. At other times he shows us how his sustaining grace enables us to endure situations that otherwise would crush us. Sometimes he makes us feel his strengthening arm upholding us in the trial. At other times he teaches us to walk by faith, believing that his arm is there even though we don't feel it. It is in these varied circumstances that we learn of his greatness, his sustaining grace, and his ability to glorify himself in ways we would never have imagined.

We think that compliant children will best teach us about his grace and the gospel, and they can. Compliant, believing children are frequently reflections of his great kindness. But the Lord also teaches us of his grace and the gospel through difficult children. We learn what it is like to love like he loved. We learn how to walk in his footsteps, and it is there, in our personal "upper room," where we learn how to wash the feet of those who are betraying us. It is there, kneeling before our rebellious children, that the real power of God is demonstrated. The compliant child's life lies to us, assuring us that she is good because we're such good parents. Difficult children tell us the truth: God loves his enemies, and he can infuse us with grace that will make us lay down our lives for them too. Their rebellion is a verification of the gospel: we produce sinful children because we are sinners, but God loves sinners. God's power is displayed through our failures when we tether ourselves to the gospel message of sin and forgiveness, no matter how desperate the situation becomes.

Content for the Sake of Christ

"For the sake of Christ, then, I am content with weaknesses, insults, hardships, persecutions, and calamities. For when I am weak, then I am strong" (2 Cor. 12:10). Paul encourages us to move past simply putting up with our difficulties to being content in them. "Content" here doesn't mean that Paul merely disciplined himself to respond with a stoic apathy: "Oh, well, I guess it's for the best." No, the word that Paul uses here is so much richer, so much more colorful than that. It means that he "takes pleasure in" or "approves" of these things. Paul doesn't simply boast about his weaknesses; no, they please him. In fact, his word, "content," is the same word that the Father uses of the Son when he declares that he is "well pleased" with him (Matt. 3:17; 12:18; 17:5; Mark 1:11; Luke 3:22). Paul's weaknesses, insults, hardships, persecutions, and calamities made Paul smile. Why? Why would Paul welcome weakness and calamity? Paul is content with these things for the "sake of Christ."

Paul's entire life was focused on proclaiming one reality: Jesus Christ and him crucified. He didn't have any other agenda, no other desire except that his life would display the glorious gospel message. He also believed that God ruled sovereignly over every aspect of his life, so he saw every trial, every betrayal and desertion, and all his weakness as God's giving him another opportunity to learn about him and rejoice in him before a watching world. That's how he could make statements like these:

Now as always Christ will be honored in my body, whether by life or by death. (Phil. 1:20)

Imprisonment and afflictions await me. But I do not account my life of any value nor as precious to myself, if only I may finish my course and the ministry that I received from the Lord Jesus, to testify to the gospel of the grace of God. (Acts 20:23–24)

I am ready not only to be imprisoned but even to die in Jerusalem for the name of the Lord Jesus. (Acts 21:13)

For we who live are always being given over to death for Jesus' sake, so that the life of Jesus also may be manifested in our mortal flesh. (2 Cor. 4:11)

Now I rejoice in my sufferings for your sake, and in my flesh I am filling up what is lacking in Christ's afflictions for the sake of his body, that is, the church. (Col. 1:24)

In responding in this way to his afflictions, Paul was following in the footsteps of his dear Savior, who confessed as he faced the cross, "Now is my soul troubled. And what shall I say? 'Father, save me from this hour'? But for this purpose I have come to this hour. Father, glorify your name" (John 12:27–28).

Father, Glorify Your Name

Are you willing to pray that your Father would glorify his name in your life, in your children's lives, no matter what the cost? Are you willing to smile at every weakness and calamity if it means that the power of Christ rests on you and the Father is glorified? We know that these are troubling questions. They trouble us too. So we throw ourselves on the mercy of God and plead that he will give us grace in every trial. We trust that he will open our eyes to the joy that awaits us when all of the benefits of his life, death, and resurrection will be ours.

We accept that weakness and affliction is the milieu in which we now live. But it won't always be like this, because although Jesus was "crucified in weakness" he now "lives by the power of God" (2 Cor. 13:4). The seeming triumph of our enemy over all that we love is not the end of our story. We are living between two worlds, between the "already" and the "not yet." Has he already triumphed victoriously over all our enemies? Yes! Will he bring all of his children safely home to him? Yes, of course!

The pastor to the Hebrews assures us that the Father has put everything in subjection to Jesus, leaving "nothing outside his control" (Heb. 2:8). Do we now see everything in subjection to him? No, "but we see him who for a little while was made lower than the angels, namely Jesus, crowned with glory and honor because of the suffering of death" (v. 9). We admit that we don't see everything coming together as we think it should for his glory right now. Not we or our parenting or our children seem to be completely submitted to his rule. But with the eyes of faith we *can* see him.

"Though you have not seen him, you love him. Though you do not now see him, you believe in him and rejoice with joy that is inexpressible and filled with glory, obtaining the outcome of your faith, the salvation of your souls" (1 Pet. 1:8–9).

We are telling you to embrace your weakness and the difficulties of parenting because they are the means that the Lord will use to acquaint you with the realities of his gracious power. But this weakness and affliction isn't all there is. No, today we can "rejoice with joy that is inexpressible and filled with glory" because we believe that he has saved our souls and that he is powerful enough to save our children's souls too.

So, go ahead. Work at being a successful parent. Manage, nurture, train, and correct your children in faith today. Teach them of God's precious promises that are able to transform their hearts. Pray for their salvation and that they would come to know and believe the love that he has for them. But hold all your labors, all your prayers, and all your plans *very loosely*. And make it your overriding desire that the Father would be glorified in every aspect of your life, whichever way he turns it. Perhaps his plan is for your family to be a wonderful example of his grace because you have respectful, obedient children. Perhaps his plan won't look anything like that. Perhaps his plan will be weakness, persecution, calamity, affliction. But whatever his plan is for you, you can rest in the assurance that he will *always* strengthen you by his grace and for his glory.

Remembering God's Grace

Please don't ignore what the Holy Spirit might be doing in your heart through this chapter. Do take the time to think deeply about it and answer the questions.

1) How does your being weak glorify your heavenly Father?
2) How can we encourage ourselves and our children when we encounter sin or weakness in our hearts?
3) Have you ever considered boasting in your weakness? How would this change the way you view yourself and your children?

4) If you have a difficult or unrepentant child, how does the perspective of boasting in weakness keep you close to Jesus?

5) Why is it good for us to see that we are weak in our parenting? What is our only hope for our children and ourselves?

6) Is it difficult or frightening for you to pray that God would glorify himself in your life however he sees fit? Why?

7) Summarize in three or four sentences what you have learned in this chapter.

10

Resting in Grace

Therefore, there will be no rest for my bones or yours unless we listen to the Word of grace and stick to it consistently and faithfully.
~ **MARTIN LUTHER**[1]

It had already been a really hard morning. Her husband had left for work in a huff, a combination of his worry about changes at his job and the general chaos that was endemic to clothing and feeding seven people in their cramped 1.5-bathroom house. In addition, it had started to snow overnight. The children would probably have to stay indoors for most of the day, and her plans to clean out the hall closet were going to have to be put on hold again. And now the two older boys were fighting again, her eldest was asleep on the couch *again*, and the toddler was crying because she'd spilled her juice all over her princess dress—*again*.

Her head ached, and she felt chilled and wondered if this was the beginning of another bout with the flu. *Give them grace? Hah!* Grace was the farthest thing from her mind! At this point, she'd be happy to simply make it through the next fifteen minutes without giving way to her frustration and despair, let alone giving them anything else aside from well-deserved timeouts in different corners of the house. *When do I get my timeout? What I would give for fifteen minutes of peace and quiet in a corner!*

Does your heart resonate with that story? No matter how disciplined, organized, and faithful we are, the reality is that we are sinners living in a sin-cursed world with other sinners. Nothing we can do will ever change that reality. We are surrounded by the realities of moths, rust, and thieves

(Matt. 6:19), Jesus's candid diagnosis of our condition. Yes, all things need to be made new, but we are not the ones who will accomplish that renovation (Rev. 21:3–5). We are exiles and strangers who see the promises from afar and believe them (Heb. 11:13), but we are walking by faith now, not by sight.

Yes, a new day when everything will be put to rights will come, but in the meantime, while we're living in the *not yet*, we need grace. And we don't need it just a tiny bit; no, the truth is we are desperate for buckets of it. We need it every hour of every day. We need it when we remember that we need it and we need it when all we can see before us is futility and trouble and disappointment. We need grace. So, now we are going to take some time to share some gracious thoughts together, before we bring our time to an end.

Since you have made it all the way to this final chapter, we assume that you are serious about trying to understand how the gospel of God's grace shapes parenting. We know that you want to give your children grace just the same way that we want to give it to our own children and grandchildren. We know that you long to share God's story with them and watch his grace transform them. We know you love them and want what is best for them and that you are committed to doing the hard work he has called you to do.

Responding to Grace

Perhaps some of you are really overjoyed about what you've read and can already feel the load of guilt and fear sliding away. To know that the Lord loves us and uses us for his glory and that he can save our children *in spite of* our parenting rather than *because of it* may have been very good news to your burdened soul. God's grace has brought sweet refreshment for your dry soul, and now you're beginning to really rest in it. Sure, you know you don't get it all the time, and you know that that is the point—you need a Savior and you have one. Whew!

We also know that there are some others who only wish that what we're saying were true. *You mean I can stop doing and doing and doing and rest in God's grace and sovereignty alone? That sounds great, but I don't think I can let myself believe it. What about . . . and what about . . . and . . . ?* We know that's a common response, because we've had that conversation with so many parents. They would like to believe that they can relax and trust the Lord—if only they could be sure that they are being responsible enough.

They have a thousand scenarios they want us to work through with them. *Yes, but what if she never prays? What if he doesn't ask for forgiveness?* and *What if . . . ? What if . . . ?*

Their love for their children coupled with fear makes them want a guaranteed method of handling every situation with complete certainty. They are serious about being godly parents, and they really don't want to give themselves a pass if resting in grace somehow means that they aren't holding up their part of the bargain. They need grace to believe that there is no bargain, because if there were, they would never be able to uphold their part of it no matter how hard they try. No bargains, no meritorious works, just grace. Remember, parenting is not a covenant of works.

Recently I was having a conversation with a mom who is trying to wrestle through the implications of grace in her parenting methods and responsibilities. She admitted that she had read too many books. She had exhausted herself trying to be a good mom and meet all the needs of all her children, raising them for the Lord. She had thought that there was a bargain. So she homeschooled and baked bread and made their clothes. They avoided television. They read books only from the 1800s. Now, in the middle of all her pain and exhaustion, she's trying to embrace grace but continues to be crippled by fear and guilt. "I wish I had never read those books," she admitted. "I feel guilty and exhausted all the time." I asked her, "How would you raise your children if all you had was the Bible?" "Well, I guess I would love them, discipline them, and tell them about Jesus." I smiled and answered, "Right."

Books, Books, and More Books

In all the centuries since the founding of the church, parents have raised children using only the Bible. Really, up until modern times with the invention of printing presses and the conveniences of modern publishing, parents had only their own parents, their community, and the church to rely on. As recently as the 1940s and 1950s, parents didn't invest time learning new methods to produce successful children, because aside from an exception or two, there really weren't any books to be had on the topic. You certainly couldn't buy books on the latest methods to get your child into shape at your local Wal-Mart. In fact, until Dr. Benjamin Spock's seminal book, *Baby and Child Care*, came out in 1946, parents simply raised their children pretty much the way they themselves had been raised. They loved them and disciplined them, and if they were believers, they told them about Jesus.

Even as recently as the decade from 1950 to 1960, there were few books or pamphlets published by Christians on parenting. Believing parents didn't go looking for the secret of successful families. They just loved their children, disciplined them, and told them about Jesus. They didn't look for anything else. They expected that parenting was going to be difficult and that children don't always turn out the way one would hope, but they assumed that they would make it through and their kids would be okay.

Just to give you a perspective on where we are today, a search on Amazon of Christian parenting books published from 1970 to 2010 produced 2,150 results. *In 2009 alone there were 142 books!* This doesn't take into account all the hundreds of books written by non-Christians about everything from what to feed your child to ensure that he'll never be fat to how to boost your child's scores on S.A.T.'s so that she'll get into the best colleges. What has been the result of this proliferation of parenting materials? Are we producing better children? Are parents and children happier, more godly? Do our kids love the gospel more?

Yes, we realize that our book adds one more to that ever-growing pile. We hope we are not being disingenuous by critiquing the number of books about parenting. We love books. We are glad that the Lord gives wisdom to Christian brothers and sisters to share with others. The writing, publishing, and reading of books is not wrong. We are thankful for all the books we've read that have made the truths of the gospel more precious, more applicable, more dear. We are thankful for every Christian writer who has poured hours into writing helpful books. Yes, we are thankful—*unless those books obscure the truth of the gospel of grace.*

How could a Christian book on parenting obscure the message of the gospel of grace? It could do so if it falsely claims that parents are able to manufacture their child's ultimate success by sheer force of will. Of course, in these books, this sheer force of will won't be called "your force of will." Rather, it will be called other, more spiritual-sounding names like "meeting their deepest needs" or "consistent" or "devoted" parenting. You'll know that a book is wandering away from grace if you read words about parenting such as:

If your [parenting] is wrong—you better get it right fast. Or you could miss your chance to meet their deepest emotional needs. Discover how to express unconditional feelings of respect, affection, and commitment that will reso-nate in their souls— and inspire them for the rest of their lives.[2]

Do you hear the underlying message of that best-selling book? Your child's success depends entirely on your ability to communicate to him in the right way. "If we do our job right as parents to instill these values, our kids will be a *success* at whatever they do! We'll have trophy kids!"[3] This is the message of every book about parenting that is not rooted in the grace of God demonstrated in the gospel. Just as a book on prayer would not be an essentially Christian book if it never mentioned Jesus's high priestly media-tion or the deep assurance that forgiveness of sins brings, so "Christian" parenting books are not Christian if their primary message is law. If their message isn't rooted and grounded in the truth that you and your children are deeply sinful yet deeply loved, in reality it's nothing more than a glori-fication of the will and work of the parent. Aside from placing a crushing burden of guilt and fear upon the backs of dads and moms, the thought that we can change anyone's heart is laughable. Change our children's hearts? Only God has power to change the heart!

Many conscientious parents have bought so deeply into these faux-Christian methods that they are utterly terrified when they hear that they need to stop trying to manipulate their children by prescribed methods. God is in control, and they can (and should) let go and trust him to guide them and save their children. How desperately we all need to remember that there are only two verses in the New Testament about Christian parenting. Only two! When we make parenting more complex than God has made it, we afflict ourselves with burdens too heavy for us to carry, and we are unin-tentionally presuming that the good news of the gospel is insufficient.

Remembering the Gospel of Grace—Again

Further, we know that sometimes it is nearly impossible to remember the gospel at all, let alone think about ways to bestow it on our children. *Jesus? The cross? What?* And then, when we find ourselves floundering without a clue, we are overcome with guilt because we aren't living up to our own expectations. *I thought that understanding the gospel of grace and how it applies to parenting would transform me, but here I am forgetting what he's done and being the same old me again!* When we forget the gospel and then feel guilty about it, we are completely missing the point of the gospel. Our ultimate joy as parents is not dependent on our ability to parent well. God's smile on us is not contingent upon anything other than the record of the beloved Son. It is based on our belief that Jesus has already done it all perfectly for us. Grace simply means resting in Jesus's blood and righteousness.

If you resonated with the little scenario with which we opened this chapter, we want you to know that you also need grace. Giving kids grace is not a new gimmick, a secret key that will automatically unlock the door to a life carefree and manageable. It won't ensure that your children will be godly, nor will it make your spouse instantly more helpful when juice cups topple. It's not something that you will always remember, nor will you understand how it applies in every situation, even when you do remember it. *Grace is God's favor given to you because of Jesus Christ, not because of your consistent memory of it.* Grace is not a thing. It is not a substance that can be measured or a commodity to be distributed. It is the "grace of the Lord Jesus Christ" (2 Cor. 13:14). In essence, it is Jesus Himself.[4]

Grace is demonstrated in the life, death, resurrection, and ascension of Jesus Christ accomplished for you. It is all that he was, is, and ever will be. He loved perfectly in your place. He obeyed consistently. He always remembered. He ever lives now as your faithful brother and High Priest, interceding for you. Jesus Christ himself is God's grace to you. He is the door that opens up access to your loving Father's heart. Grace is what he has given to you: it is that oh-so-costly unmerited favor. And with that favor comes his strength to enable you to persevere through every trial of parenting. Grace is not a novel, failsafe catchphrase that will ensure successful parenting. No, it's something so much better than that! It is *God's assured favorable attitude toward undeserving rebels whom, in his inscrutable love, he has decided to bless.*

When he looks with favor upon us as beloved children, he also supplies the strength or grace we need to persevere through every trial of life, whether or not we remember his grace. Grace isn't created by our ability to work at it or even remember it—that's why it's called "grace." Paul makes this point abundantly clear when writing to the Romans about his saved Jewish kinsmen who were "chosen by grace. But if it is by grace, it is no longer on the basis of works; otherwise grace would no longer be grace"

(Rom. 11:5–6). Parenting in grace is not parenting on the basis of your own consistent gospel-centeredness. It is just the opposite. Parenting in grace is parenting on the basis of Christ's consistent perfections *alone*.

Growing in Grace

None of us, not even the authors of this book, know everything we will one day know about grace. We, too, frequently forget the gospel and quickly slip back into methods of parenting that are driven by anything but the gospel. But we're not alone in our deficiency in understanding and apprehending grace, which is why Peter wrote these words about grace that function as bookends to his second letter: "May grace and peace be multiplied to you in the knowledge of God and of Jesus our Lord" (2 Pet. 1:2). He also wrote, "But grow in the grace and knowledge of our Lord and Savior Jesus Christ. To him be the glory both now and to the day of eternity. Amen" (2 Pet. 3:18).

Can you see how growing in grace is in some ways synonymous with growing in our knowledge of the gospel? In other words, the more time we spend pondering what Jesus has already done for us, the more we will grow in comprehending grace, that we have been highly favored by what Jesus has done. This understanding will eventually transform how we parent our children. We will favor them with our love and attention because we will see how we have been so abundantly favored. We will be conscious of our sin when we see theirs, and we will stop trying to preserve our great reputation as parents. We will be patient because he has been so patient with us. We will really love because we've been really loved. This understanding of the foundation of grace will *slowly* transform our expectations, hopes, and desires for ourselves and our children. Grace changes everything about us—even when we forget it.

Grace transforms our parenting because it makes our sin immense in our eyes by showing us the hideousness of the bloody cross that was necessary before God could favor us with forgiveness. Every sin we've committed as parents was placed upon him there. Grace makes mercy huge because it reveals the price he had to pay to bestow that grace on us. We deserved judgment; we've been given mercy! It magnifies God's great mercies because we see the unimaginable suffering of the Son who fulfilled all righteousness (Matt. 3:15) and was forsaken (Matt. 27:46). Grace magnifies Jesus Christ and shows us our weakness and dependency.

So, when you have that morning to top all mornings, when everything that could possibly go wrong does, when grace doesn't mean anything to you, it is his grace that will sustain you. What mornings like these teach us is that we're just like our children. They forget, and so do we. They need grace, and so do we. We are partners in grace with them.

Humble Partners in Grace

When we're feeling our weakest and really don't have any idea how grace or the gospel might apply in a particular situation (and are not sure if we care), we'll know that it's okay to be silent and simply wait. Many times, our children don't understand the gospel or grace either. We don't need to try to drum up some gospel speech that isn't resonating within our hearts to be sure we've got our bases covered. We are partners with our children because we are just like them—dearly loved sinners. It will comfort their souls when they see that there isn't something intrinsically wrong with them because they don't understand the gospel all the time.

Conversely, it's when we get so wrapped up in whether we are saying the right thing at the right time and trying to see into their hearts to be sure that there is some sort of faith or change that we become afraid of making mistakes, and we fall back into self-reliance. When we think that everything is up to us, we won't see how we are to partner with them as beloved fellow sinners. Instead, we will mistakenly assume that it's up to us to make them believe and change their hearts. We can't get at their hearts. We can't even get at our own (Jer. 17:5).

Partnering in grace with our children means that we are together learning to rely on the Holy Spirit. Telling our children that we, too, are struggling to understand how the gospel can change us and admitting we really don't see how it does right now will teach them that faith doesn't mean that we have certainty or clarity all the time. Sometimes we will simply need to manage them while we wait for light. At times like this we can honestly tell them that we are trying to see what the gospel looks like and that we are walking in shadow.

This place of transparency and brokenness before our children and the Lord will ultimately be a place of freedom and grace, even though at first it will feel like a place of despair and humiliation. When we really understand that there is nothing we can say or do that will change our children's hearts, at that moment we're in the place of humility that is the *only* door to promised grace.

> Clothe yourselves, all of you, with humility toward one another, for "God opposes the proud but gives grace to the humble." Humble yourselves, therefore, under the mighty hand of God so that at the proper time he may exalt you, casting all your anxieties on him, because he cares for you. Be sober-minded; be watchful. Your adversary the devil prowls around like a roaring lion, seeking someone to devour. Resist him, firm in your faith, knowing that the same kinds of suffering are being experienced by your brotherhood throughout the world. And after you have suffered a little while, the God of all grace, who has called you to his eternal glory in Christ, will himself restore, confirm, strengthen, and establish you. To him be the dominion forever and ever. Amen. (1 Pet. 5:5–11)

Although God has promised to resist parents who proudly assume they can save the day by their own efforts, he has also promised to give grace to those who humbly bow before him, casting all their cares on him and admitting their weaknesses and poverty. Only humility, only transparent confession of our great need, will result in the grace we so desperately need to parent the little fellow sinners in our home.

We will never be able to love them as we should. And even though there are only two commands in the New Testament about parenting, we will never raise them in the nurture and admonition of the Lord. Not perfectly, never consistently. Our job is not just hard; *it's impossible*. It is at those moments, when we're struck dumb by our failure and unbelief and brokenly fall on our knees before him, that his promised grace is most powerful in us. When we are feeling total despair, when we think, *I'm never going to get this right, and even when I try, I fail*, that will be the moment when we'll have the grace to resist our enemy and watch how our Savior restores, confirms, strengthens, and establishes us.

We need days of failure because they help humble us, and through them we can see how God's grace is poured out on the humble. It is on days like this that the words, "The God of all grace, who has called you to his eternal glory in Christ" (1 Pet. 5:10), will bring deep comfort and great joy to your soul. *Oh, Lord, I can't see you now, and I feel so weak and inadequate, but you've promised that we'll be together in your eternal glory in Christ. Lord Jesus, I thank you and humble myself before you. Please help me see and believe.*

It is in times of humility, of saying that we're in great need, that his grace is promised to us. Do you feel the need for more grace to love your children and see the gospel in your daily life with them? Then rest in his arms and admit your brokenness. He has promised and he is always faithful to keep his promises.

Dazzle Them with the Gospel of Grace

The one thing that our children really need is the gospel of grace. They need to be absolutely dazzled by the kind of love that would suffer the way Christ suffered, forgive the way he forgives, and bless the way he blesses. Martin Luther wrote that it is grace that brings us forgiveness of sins, which produces peace of conscience. The words are simple; but during temptation, "to be convinced in our hearts that we have forgiveness of sins and peace with God by grace alone is the hardest thing."[5]

Living and parenting in grace is not the easy road. In fact, it is much harder to rest in his promise of grace than it is to make a list and try to live by it. Some parents may think that giving grace to their children equates to giving themselves a pass. Just the opposite is true. Giving grace to children is an exercise of faith, and faith is always more difficult than works. It flows out of humility, a character trait that none of us comes by naturally. That's why most people miss it and why works, not faith, is the stumbling block of the cross. You are not slacking off when you tell them of his dazzling love. You are doing the hardest thing.

So go ahead. Freely dazzle your babies with the cross of Christ. Give them grace when they succeed and grace when they fail. Show them how much he loves little children, like you. Bring them to him and encourage them to jump up on his lap and share all their silly stories and fears and joys with him. Assure them of his great delight in them. And when they sin, when they fail, tell them all over again, "Oh, honey. Let's run to our Savior. Jesus loves sinners. Let's tell him about our sin and ask him for grace to love him even more." Then, when you give them grace like this, you'll find yourself dazzled by his love and grace, too.

Remembering God's Grace

Please don't ignore what the Holy Spirit might be doing in your heart through this chapter. Do take the time to think deeply about it and answer the questions.

1) How does the grace God has shown us completely change the way we parent?
2) How does the grace God has shown us help us in our failures as parents?
3) How does the grace God has shown us help us see our successes as parents?
4) How can you now partner with your child in the gospel?
5) Summarize in three or four sentences what you have learned in this chapter.

Remembering God's Grace One More Time

Why not take time now to think about and write out what the Lord has taught you through this study?

1) What have you learned about the gospel of grace?

2) Review the answers you wrote to the questions at the end of earlier chapters. Would you answer them differently now?

3) What have you learned about yourself?

4) What have you learned about parenting?

5) What are you hoping that the Lord will help you change in your life?

6) How has Jesus become sweeter to you through this study? Stop to pray now that the Holy Spirit will enable you to share this sweetness with your family.

Appendix 1

The One Good Story

Once upon a time, long, long ago, there was a great king who ruled in perfect happiness over all his kingdom. Because this kingdom was so wonderful, so beautiful, everyone who lived in it was always happy. No one was ever sad; no one ever had to be told to obey, because everyone loved the king and the king loved all his subjects.

This wonderful king also had a son whom he loved very dearly. The son always did whatever his father wanted him to do because he loved his father so much and knew that everything his father wanted him to do was good and would make him really happy. For years and years they lived in utter pleasure and contentment.

Then one day the father said to the son, "I would like you to have a bride and to know the joy of giving yourself away. Do you want to give yourself like this, even though you are perfectly content and happy here?" "Yes, dear father, I would love to have a bride and serve her." So a plan was made.

Together the father and the son went to a far corner of their kingdom and chose a bride for the son's joy. But there was a terrible problem in the place where his bride lived: even though she owed all her allegiance to the great king, she had fallen under the spell of a wicked imposter who hated the king and held her captive. Although her slavery was harsh and brutal, she had foolishly chosen to serve this evil one rather than journey toward the good king in obedience. The more she sought to satisfy the wicked imposter's demands, the more he enslaved her and put terrible, painful burdens on her back.

In her misery she purposely did things the great king had told her not to do, just to try to prove she wasn't a slave. At other times she tried to be very good to prove that she really didn't need the king after all. This disobedience only made her life more miserable, but still she stubbornly refused to send messages to the king for help. But that didn't stop the great king. He loved her anyway, and even though she refused to ask him for help, help was already on the way. The beloved son was coming to rescue her.

Because he was so wise, the beloved son knew that if he arrived for his bride arrayed in his royal robes and with his army, his bride would be terrified of him. He also knew that in order to rescue her, he would have to suffer just like she did. So, instead of appearing like a mighty prince on a stallion, he disguised himself so that he looked just like her. His disguise was so good that at first she didn't recognize him. He looked just like any other servant of the evil imposter. But the more she heard what he said and watched what he did, the more she could tell that there was something very different about him. Unlike the wicked imposter, he was gentle and loving when she failed. When she was with him, she began to feel that there was hope to be free from the wicked imposter's grasp; in fact, being with him actually started to make her love the great king again. Even though she was changing, she still didn't realize that he was the great king's son.

But the wicked imposter knew who the beloved son was. He recognized him because he had known him long ago, before he had rebelled and been evicted from the beautiful kingdom. Now this imposter hated the great king even more and was furious at the thought that he was going to take away his slaves and punish him for his mutiny. So he schemed to try to find a way to trap the beloved son and hurt him.

At first the wicked imposter promised the son all sorts of presents if the son would just join him in his rebellion against the great king. But the beloved son refused; he knew that the imposter's so-called presents would only poison him and make him sad. The dark pretender couldn't fool him. So in furious anger he did the most terrible thing that has ever been done. He fooled some of his servants so that they rose up against the son. He got them to pretend that they were serving the great king, and they accused the son of saying things about himself and the king that were not true.

Of course, any time he wanted to, the son could have shown them who he really was, but this wasn't part of his father's plan. No, in the father's plan the beloved son would have to die for his bride's foolishness and evil. So the son hid his real power and allowed himself to be mistreated so she could escape the imposter's grasp. Then the most terrible thing of all happened: the people killed the beloved son! Of course, the wicked imposter fooled them into thinking they were really serving the great king by doing this terrible thing. While they were foolishly scoffing at his suffering, all the other creatures in the kingdom wept in great sorrow at this scandalous sight. Everything that they had ever known was suddenly changed. The beloved son had been killed! He was dead!

In most stories, next would come two words: "The End." But this story isn't like other stories. This story is very different. This is the best story you've ever heard. You have to remember that this great king owned everything and had the power and right to do whatever he wanted. He wanted his son to be happy with his new bride (even though she had just killed him), so after a few days, he brought his beloved son back to life again. The beloved son had taken the punishment for all the bad things that his bride had ever done, and his father had taken the record for all the good things that his son had ever done and given it to his bride. This was the greatest wedding present anyone had ever given. All the good went to the bride and all the bad went to her beloved husband. Have you ever heard a story like this before?

By the great king's power, the beloved son was breathing again. He ate fish and talked with his friends. He was alive! Then, after forty days, the beloved son went back to his father's home. Can you imagine how glad they were to be together again? For the rest of time, they would never really be apart. But the son who came back to the great king's house had changed. Now, he looked exactly like his bride except for one thing: he had marks on his body that proved that he had suffered for her and bought the right to have her for his own. Those marks were kind of like his wedding ring; they reminded him, and her too, of what he had suffered for her and how much he loved her.

From then on he would look like her and watch over her and protect her from the wicked imposter's tricks. Then, when it was time, he would send a messenger to bring her home to him. He made a promise never to leave her alone and to one day reclaim all the kingdom that the wicked imposter had tried to grab from him. Even though not everyone knew what the beloved son had done, someday they would all know and worship him.

This is the best story that was ever told because unlike other good stories, this story will change you if you believe it. This story is like a door, because if you believe that the story is true, a door into the beloved Son's kingdom will open to you, and you'll be able to walk through it.

Appendix 2

Common Problems and the Gospel

In the charts on the following pages you'll find eight common problems that parents face. We have given you a way to respond to each problem with Management, Nurturing, Training, Correcting and remembering the Promises of the gospel—MNTCP.

These examples are meant to aid you in understanding how the gospel informs and transforms responses to the typical difficulties parents face every day. They are not meant to be memorized, as though they could answer every problem perfectly. They are just there so you can begin to understand the concepts we have presented throughout this book in a more concrete way.

As we have said before, don't try to apply every one, every time. This isn't a formula; it's a way of thinking. Please remember also that one of the most important responses, when you're faced with a greedy, complaining, or lazy child, is to pray that the Holy Spirit will help you and your kids to see how the work of Jesus Christ applies. Remember, we are relying on his grace and not on our abilities to transform our kids.

Lying

Category	Scripture	Example
Management or Oversight	Gen. 31:34–35 Ex. 20:16 Josh. 7:1, 20 Acts 5:1–11 Eph. 4:25	**Basic instructions for daily living:** "Lying is against God's law. Please tell me the truth about what happened right now."
Gospel Nurturing	Zech. 13:1 Col. 3:3	**Feeding her soul with grace:** "I see that you are afraid of being disciplined for what you just did. But lying is only going to make this situation worse for you. If you believe, Christ covered your sin with his death so that you wouldn't have to try to cover it and lie about what you have done."
Gospel Training	Isa. 53:9 Matt. 26:57–65 1 John 1:9	**What Jesus has done:** "When Jesus was brought before the judges before he was crucified, they gave him a chance to lie about who he was. If he had lied and said that he wasn't God, they wouldn't have hurt him. The Bible tells us that Jesus was sad that he was going to be punished not just by the judges but by God. He was punished by God for your sin. If he had lied, then he would not have been crucified, and he could not have paid for your sin and taken your punishment on the cross. But he didn't lie, and because he didn't lie you can have the courage to be honest and tell me what happened."
Gospel Correction	Ps. 32:5 Prov. 28:13	**Correcting her when she doubts or forgets:** "Right now, you're acting like Jesus's taking your eternal punishment isn't enough for you. You must remember that you don't have to hide your sin anymore. The cross tells me that you and I are both terrible sinners and that God himself had to die to pay for our sin. So please be honest with me about what you did. I already know that you sin; I sin too. But the Bible tells us that if we confess our sin, we are promised mercy."

Lying *contintued*

Category	Scripture	Example
Rehearsing Gospel Promises	Genesis 3 Matt. 27:11–13 John 2:24; 3:16-18; 8:24 Acts 16:31 Rom. 3:23–24; 4:22–25 1 Cor. 4:5 Heb. 4:13 Rev. 2:23	**If she isn't a Christian:** "I can see that you are afraid of being disciplined and that you don't want to be honest about what you have done. You think that lying will stop you from being punished. There is no way for me to know the truth right now because I can't force you to tell the truth. I can't see what really happened. You can hide from me and lie, and I won't know. But please hear me: God can see, and he knows. Even though you might not be punished here and now, you will receive punishment for every sin you've ever committed from the most powerful one of all. You will eventually have to be punished for your sin. But you can turn to Jesus, the one who took your eternal punishment, today." **If she is a Christian:** "Jesus Christ has paid the price for your sin of lying, He has also paid the price for whatever sin you're trying to cover up right now. The Bible calls the Devil 'The Father of Lies.' Do you know what was the first lie that Satan told? He convinced Adam and Eve that God's love wasn't enough for them. He convinced them that they needed more than God's love. Please know that every lie you tell is saying the same thing. You lie because you want to hide your sin; you don't want to be punished. But if you are in him, he has already taken the eternal punishment for you because of his love. You don't have to hide your sin; you are already hidden in him. Jesus Christ was courageous and bold when faced with the decision to lie and get out of punishment or to tell the truth and be killed. He told the truth because of his never-ending love for you. Right now he is praying for you to tell the truth. He has given you the Holy Spirit to give you the courage and grace to tell the truth."

Blame Shifting, Making Excuses

Category	Scripture	Example
Management or Oversight	Gen. 3:11–13; 4:9 I Sam. 15:20–21 Prov. 19:3 James 1:13–15	**Basic instructions for daily living:** "Please don't make any more excuses or blame your sin on anybody else right now."
Gospel Nurturing	I John 1:8–10	**Feeding his soul with grace:** "I know that it can be hard to admit that you sinned. I struggle with that sin also. But your sin is nobody's fault but yours. The good news is Jesus paid for every sin, if you believe. And you don't have to make excuses anymore. Please just accept what he has already done for you."
Gospel Training	Rom. 6:4–6, 12, 19	**What Jesus has done:** "Jesus has paid for your sin by his death on the cross. He also lived a perfect life in your place, so now you don't have to pretend you are perfect anymore. What Jesus has done for you tells us both that you are not perfect, but he loves you anyway."
Gospel Correction	2 Cor. 7:1	**Correcting him when he doubts or forgets:** "Right now you're acting like what Jesus has done for you isn't enough. You're acting like your reputation is all that matters. You know that even if everybody thought you were perfect and that nothing was your fault, it wouldn't make you happy. Here is the good news: God has given you and me Jesus Christ's reputation. He has given you his record of always doing what is right. So you don't have to try to make me think you always do what is right. Please stop making excuses and be honest about your sin and about who you are. The truth is you are more sinful than you can ever know, but you are also more loved than you could ever imagine."

Blame Shifting, Making Excuses *continued*

Category	Scripture	Example
Rehearsing Gospel Promises	Eccles. 11:9 Matt. 12:36 Rom. 14:12 Gal. 3:11 Titus 3:4–7	**If he isn't a Christian:** "I understand why you are trying to justify yourself and what you have done. It is because what others think of you and what you think of yourself are all that matters. When you stand before God, you will not be able to make any excuse that will fix how you have lived. But you can turn to him today." **If he is a Christian:** "Do you know what the word *justified* means? It means that God sees you just as if you had never sinned. He sees you the way you are trying to get me to see you right now. But that isn't all: he also looks at you just as if you always obeyed. Can you believe that? His amazing love for you caused him to send Jesus Christ to earth and to live a perfect life and take your punishment so that you will be justified before him. You don't have to blame your sin on anybody else. You don't have to make excuses for what you have done. All you have to do is remember what he has done for you and freely admit you need his record. You need him to live and die for you. You need him to do it all for you, and if you truly believe, he has."

Disobeying

Category	Scripture	Example
Management or Oversight	Ex. 20:12 Eph. 6:1	**Basic instructions for daily living:** "Right now you need to do what I am asking. Please stop what you are doing and do what I have told you to do."
Gospel Nurturing	Luke 22:42 James 4:6 1 Pet. 5:5	**Feeding her soul with grace:** "I can see that you want to do your own thing right now. I see that what I have asked you to do is not important. I understand wanting my own way. But Christ will give you grace to help you obey even though you don't want to. He understands obeying even when it is hard. Please ask him to help you obey now and remember that he always obeyed perfectly in your place."
Gospel Training	Heb. 5:7–10; 10:5–10	**What Jesus has done:** "Jesus obeyed in the most difficult circumstances; he did this because he loves you, and because he wants to pour his love out on you. Now, because he obeyed perfectly, you can ask him to help you obey. He understands what it is like to have to do something difficult."
Gospel Correction	Phil. 2:1–11 Heb. 12:1–3	**Correcting her when she doubts or forgets:** "When you disobey, you are saying that what you want is more important than anything else. You have forgotten the most important thing of all: Jesus Christ was obedient unto death for the joy set before him. Do you know what that joy was? The joy that was set before him was redeeming you. Please see and know this love. His obedience is the most beautiful, important, satisfying thing in the world. As you lift your eyes to his obedience, you will be able to obey."

Disobeying *continued*

Category	Scripture	Example
Rehearsing Gospel Promises	Gen. 6:5 Luke 2:52 Rom. 13:1 Phil. 2:10–11 Heb. 4:15	**If she isn't a Christian:** "I can see how you think that the only thing that will make you happy is to do what you want to do. Living for yourself and what you want will never satisfy you. For the rest of your life, you will be called to obey authority. If you don't learn this now, it will be hard for you for your entire life. And please know that there will be a day when you will obey God, and on that day your knee will bow and your tongue will confess that he is Lord. On that day it will be too late to try and obey, but you can turn to him today." **If she is a Christian:** "Do you know that you have Christ's perfect record of always obeying? Do you see how amazing that is right this second? You don't want to obey; your heart is actually set to disobey me. Even though you know you should obey, you have decided that what you want is more important than doing what God has called you to do. But here is the good news: Jesus Christ always obeyed his parents in your place. Can you imagine always knowing the best way to do things, knowing the easiest, smartest way to do everything, but then having to obey what someone else said? Jesus Christ submitted to his parents so that right now you would have his perfect record of obedience. He not only submitted to his parents who loved him, but he also submitted to the rulers of his age who hated him. It would be so hard to obey someone who hates you, and lies about you, and wants to kill you, especially if you knew he was completely wrong. But he did obey, he obeyed so that he could make you his child. He is the perfect Father to you, who always loves you and always wants what is best for you. He has put me in your life to protect and help you to learn to obey."

Provoking Others

Category	Scripture	Example
Management or Oversight	Rom. 1:32 1 Cor. 13:6 Eph. 4:32 Phil. 1:18–19	**Basic instructions for daily living:** "You are being unkind right now. Please stop provoking your sister."
Gospel Nurturing	Isa. 53:3–5	**Feeding his soul with grace:** "I see that right now you are enjoying hurting your sister. You think your joy is going to come from controlling your sister's emotions by making her angry. Jesus Christ was hurt for your sake. He was beaten and bruised so that your sin of unkindness could be forgiven. Please ask him to help you learn to love the way you have been loved."
Gospel Training	Isa. 53:6–8 Matt. 20:28	**What Jesus has done:** "The entire time Jesus was here on earth he was mistreated, hurt, and rejected so that he could show his amazing love to you. The way you are tempting your sister to sin in anger right now is the very sin that he had to die for."
Gospel Correction	Matt. 27:27–31 Rom. 5:15–21	**Correcting him when he doubts or forgets:** "Right now you're acting like Jesus's love for you isn't enough. By hurting your sister, you are saying that you need more than Jesus's love to make you happy. You are saying that you need to control someone else to be happy. Do you know that Jesus was hurt so that you could be happy? There is only true happiness in his love for you—his love that caused him to hurt. When you see his remarkable love for you, you can love your sister even when you don't feel like it."

Provoking Others *continued*

Category	Scripture	Example
Rehears-ing Gospel Promises	John 8:34–36; 10:15–17 Rom. 6:6 Gal. 5:13–25 Heb. 2:11 1 John 3:16	**If he isn't a Christian:** "I can see that you are enjoying hurting your sister right now. You are enjoying the control you have over her. Please understand that the control you are enjoying will trap you. You will love trying to control people, you will love the power you have over people, you will love hurting people, and then one day you will see that you actually have no control at all. The most powerful one who ever existed will have control over how you spend eternity, and you will be called to account for every temptation to sin you placed before your sister. But you can turn to Jesus today." **If he is a Christian:** "Right now you are trying to control your sister by hurting her. You are enjoying the anger and pain she is experiencing. You are forgetting that God promises to control you with his love. Jesus Christ was hurt so that you could be loved. The people that were hurting him thought they were controlling what was going on. They thought they were taking his life from him. The Bible tells us that he was actually in control of his death. It says that he willingly laid his life down. Now we can be controlled by his love. Now he looks at you and sees a perfect record of always being loving and kind to everyone. He always loved his siblings perfectly. God sees Jesus's perfect record of being a perfect brother. Jesus is your perfect brother, treating you with love and kindness. Please remember this and give up trying to hurt and control your sister."

Fighting/Anger

Category	Scripture	Example
Management or Oversight	James 4:2, 4 1 John 3:12	**Basic instructions for daily living:** "You must stop fighting with your brother. "
Gospel Nurturing	Rom. 12:10 1 John 3:11–12; 4:11	**Feeding his soul with grace:** "I understand that you are very angry with your brother right now. You are so angry that you are hurting him. You are not loving your brother the way you have been loved. Jesus Christ loved you and fought to win you. Because of his love for you, you can love your brother."
Gospel Training	Luke 23:34, 39–43	**What Jesus has done:** "When Jesus was on the cross, he had people screaming at him and insulting him, and trying to fight with him. Do you know how he responded to them? He loved them. He stayed on the cross and didn't fight with them. In fact, he actually saved the soul of the one being punished next to him."
Gospel Correction	Pss. 16:11; 21:5–6 2 Cor. 4:17	**Correcting him when he doubts or forgets:** "When you fight with your friend, you are saying to God that whatever you are fighting over is more important than him and his love. If you are fighting to be heard, or to have someone tell you that you are right, or over a toy, or over being the best—whatever it is, it is truly nothing compared to the satisfaction that you can find in Christ. You are forgetting the real prize in this life. The real prize is knowing that you are loved by him."

Fighting/Anger *continued*

Category	Scripture	Example
Rehearsing Gospel Promises	Gen. 3:15 Prov. 1:16–19 Eccles. 4:8 Nah. 1:2 1 Cor. 15:51–58	**If he isn't a Christian:** "Right now you're pouring out your anger on your friend by fighting with him. You are a little boy, and your anger and strength make you feel powerful, but your strength is small compared to the God who made and sustains the entire universe. Please know that he has promised to pour his anger out on those who hate him, and those who don't turn to him to rescue them from this anger. You can turn to him today." **If he is a Christian:** "Do you know that the biggest fight in all of history has already been won? That was the fight that Jesus fought for you. He fought against Satan and he won. He conquered, completely defeated, Satan. He fought the fight to win your soul, and we should praise him for that. He gave his life during that fight; he had to die in order to win that fight. Remarkably, he did win. He died, and he won. The fight wasn't just during his death on the cross; he fought his entire life. He fought against every temptation and every sin. Every time someone was mean to him, he fought to love. That is truly the hardest thing to fight to do. But you can fight to love others too; you can fight to love because he has loved you."

Complaining

Category	Scripture	Example
Management or Oversight	Num. 14:27 Ps. 106:25 1 Cor. 10:10 Phil. 2:14	**Basic instructions for daily living:** "Complaining about what we are having for dinner is inappropriate and unloving. Please stop talking now."
Gospel Nurturing	Acts 4:24–28	**Feeding her soul with grace:** "I know that you don't like what is happening right now. I find my heart ungrateful and full of complaints all the time too. But you must remember what you have already been given. Jesus Christ is so much better than getting what you think you want right now. Please remember that every situation that comes into our lives is meant to make us more like Christ and to bring him glory. He submitted to God's sovereign plan for you."
Gospel Training	Matt. 11:25 Luke 10:21 John 11:41–42	**What Jesus has done:** "Do you know that Jesus lived a life full of perfect gratitude? He knew that the happiest way to live was by remembering that God had every situation planned to bring God glory. Because Jesus went to the cross without complaint, he died for you without complaint; you can eat your dinner remembering his amazing love for you."
Gospel Correction	Gal. 3:9 Eph. 1:3	**Correcting her when she doubts or forgets:** "I know that all you can see right now is that you're not getting what you want. I want to ask you to open your eyes to all that Christ has already given you. You have been blessed with every spiritual blessing; you have everything you need right this second."

Complaining *continued*

Category	Scripture	Example
Rehears-ing Gospel Promises	Luke 12:15–21; 16:23–30 Rom. 6:23 Phil. 3:7–10; 4:18	**If she isn't a Christian:** "The only thing that can bring you any sort of fading joy today is for you to get what you think you want. You could live your entire life trying to get what you want and becoming more and more unhappy when you don't. I can promise you that whatever you want or get here on earth will never be enough. Your life will be spent running after something that doesn't exist. There is no satisfaction without Christ; there is no joy without Christ. The only thing you will end up with is a pile of sin that has to be paid for. And please believe me when I say that someone will pay for your sin. But you can turn to him today." **If she is a Christian:** "There is no greater treasure than Christ. You want a different dinner? He is the most filling and delightful taste you will ever experience. You want new toys? He is the most exciting, enthralling pursuit you will ever know. You want people to treat you differently? He has poured out all his never-ending love on you. You already have what you are complaining that you don't have. You actually have something better than what you are striving to get right now. Please stop and pray that you can see what is yours in Christ Jesus. I assure you, you won't be disappointed."

Talking Back

Category	Scripture	Example
Management or Oversight	Ex. 20:12 Rom. 13:7	**Basic instructions for daily living:** "I am going to ask you to stop talking back to me. You need to hear what I am going to say without interrupting."
Gospel Nurturing	Ps. 71:5–6 Isa. 30:15; 32:17	**Feeding his soul with grace:** "I can see that what you think you are trying to tell me is important. I need you to hear me when I say that you need to trust God to take care of you. He understands and knows what you want to say; he knows your heart. He hears every cry of his children, and he cares deeply about all that you think you need. I need you to be quiet and just listen."
Gospel Training	Isa. 53:7 Acts 8:32 1 Pet. 2:22–25	**What Jesus has done:** "When Jesus Christ was before his accusers, before the people that hated him, he was quiet. The Bible says that he was like a lamb led to the slaughter. He didn't fight to have his opinion heard, even though his opinion was the only one that really mattered. If you are in Christ, that record is yours. Because he went silently to the cross to bear your sin, you can trust him and listen quietly to what I am going to say."
Gospel Correction	Pss. 19:14; 36:3, 5 1 Tim. 6:17–18	**Correcting him when he doubts or forgets:** "I understand that you want to get your point across to me, but I am asking you to be quiet. I know I don't see the situation perfectly, but God does. I am going to pray for wisdom, and I would like you to pray that you would trust God instead of your own opinion. Please don't talk back to me anymore, but just listen and then do what I am asking. Our heavenly Father will give us both exactly what we need right now."

Talking Back *continued*

Category	Scripture	Example
Rehears-ing Gospel Promises	Prov. 3:5–6 Matt. 6:26	**If he isn't a Christian:** "Trying to convince people that you are right and they are wrong is going to be a difficult way for you to live your life. Almost everyone out there tries to do the same thing. You will get better at arguing, but that won't bring you the justification you are looking for. The justification you are looking for is found only in Christ. If you spend your life attempting to get it by your own effort, you will stand before a holy God with nothing but your sin, and your mouth will be closed then. But you can turn to him today." **If he is a Christian:** "Please trust your heavenly Father's ability to take care of you in this situation. He has put me in your life to help you right now, and you must listen to what I have to say without interrupt-ing. His care for you is so immense that he died to make you his son. Don't trust in your ability to talk your way out of this situation; you don't need to fight the situation. Please just trust that he will help us both as we try to work this out. God has given us both these circumstances so that we can learn not to rely on our own wisdom or ability to see everything clearly, but that we would rely on him to lead us. Let's pray together that we may learn to be quiet and wait for his help."

Laziness

Category	Scripture	Example
Management or Oversight	Prov. 12:24; 19:15 2 Thess. 3:10	**Basic instructions for daily living:** "I have asked you to get off the couch and go clean your room. Please do that now."
Gospel Nurturing	Matt. 26:36–45	**Feeding her soul with grace:** "I see that you don't want to go and work right now. Please remember the incredibly difficult work Jesus did for you because he loves you. Please pray that he will help your heart to see that work and motivate you to do the work you are being asked to do now. Jesus is working even now for your benefit. He's praying for you."
Gospel Training	Ps. 22:1–2 Heb. 5:7–9	**What Jesus has done:** "The Bible tells us that Jesus wept great tears as he thought about the great work that he had to do on the cross. That work secured a position before his Father for you. What he went through on your behalf he had to do because of your love for comfort and your laziness. Please know his love for you is better than feeling comfortable right now."
Gospel Correction	Matt. 11:28–30 John 19:17–18 Heb. 12:2	**Correcting her when she doubts or forgets:** "Please see that your desire to sit there will not bring you happiness. You believe that playing on the computer is going to bring you satisfaction. I promise you it won't. The only thing that will bring you true rest is to see what has already been done for you. When you see what has been done for you, you can get up and do the work we are asking you to do."

Laziness *continued*

Category	Scripture	Example
Rehearsing Gospel Promises	Eph. 4:17–28 Col. 3:5–6 Rev. 6:16	**If she isn't a Christian:** "Your love of rest and relaxation are controlling you right now. It is honestly all you have to live for. Thinking that you deserve comfort will only cause you pain and anger for the rest of your life. God has promised to do the work of pouring out his wrath against those that love anything more than they love him. You will get exactly what you have earned on that last day. But you can turn to him today." **If she is a Christian:** "I am praying that you will see the futility in thinking that relaxation is what will bring you joy. You have been given something infinitely better than two hours of doing nothing. Jesus did everything for you so that at times when you are being asked to work and you don't want to work, you will be able to see his perfect work for you. You will see that he performed the hardest most uncomfortable work that any human has ever had to perform. He gave up his perfect place of rest and happiness in heaven to come to earth and work every day at not giving in to sin. He then went to the cross and was obedient unto death so that your laziness and lack of love for others would be totally covered by his blood. The most difficult part of the work he did for you was being separated from his Father. Our sin placed on his back separated him from the thing that brought him the most joy. He went through that so that you never have to, so that in this time of bending your will to someone else's you can remember you are not alone. He is praying for you; he walked this road before you. He understands how hard work is. He will help you."

Appendix 3

The Best News Ever

I (Elyse) didn't begin to understand the gospel until the summer before my twenty-first birthday. Although I had attended church from time to time in my childhood, I'll admit that it never really transformed me in any significant way. I was frequently taken to Sunday school where I heard stories about Jesus. I knew, without really understanding, the importance of Christmas and Easter. I remember looking at the beautiful stained-glass windows, with their cranberry red and deep cerulean blue, with Jesus knocking on a garden door, and having a vague sense that being religious was good. But I didn't have the foggiest idea about the gospel.

When adolescence came barging in, my strongest memories are those of despair and anger. I was consistently in trouble, and I hated everyone who pointed that out. There were nights when I prayed that I would be good, or more specifically, get out of whatever trouble I was in and do better, only to be disappointed and angered by the failures of the following day.

Upon graduation from high school at seventeen, I was married, had a baby, and was divorced—all before the third decade of my life began. It was during the following months and years that I discovered the anesthetizing effects of drugs, alcohol, and illicit relationships. Although I would have been known as a girl who liked to party, I was utterly lost and joyless, and I was beginning to know it.

At one point, I can remember telling a friend that I felt like I was fifty years old, which, at that point in my life, was the oldest I could imagine anyone being. I was exhausted and disgusted, so I decided to set about improving myself. I worked a full-time job, took a full load at a local junior college, and cared for my son. I changed my living arrangements and tried to start over. I didn't know that the Holy Spirit was working in my heart, calling me to the Son. I just knew that something had to change. Don't misunderstand: I was still living a shamefully wicked life; it's just that I felt like I was beginning to wake up to something different.

At this point, Julie entered my life. She was my next-door neighbor, and she was a Christian. She was kind to me, and we became fast friends. She had a quality of life about her that attracted me, and she was always talking to me about her Savior, Jesus. She let me know that she was praying for me and would frequently encourage me to "get saved." Although I'd had that Sunday school training, what she had to say was something completely different from what I'd ever remembered hearing. She told me I needed to be "born again."

So, on a warm night sometime in June of 1971, I knelt down in my tiny apartment and told the Lord that I wanted to be his. At that point, I didn't really understand much about the gospel, but I did understand this: I knew I was desperate, and I desperately believed that the Lord would help me. That prayer on that night changed everything about me. I remember it now, thirty-nine years later, as if it were yesterday.

In the words of Scripture, I knew I needed to be saved, and I trusted that he could save me. One man who came in contact with some of Jesus's followers asked this same question: "What must I do to be saved?" The answer was simple: "Believe in the Lord Jesus, and you will be saved" (Acts 16:31).

Very simply, what do you need to believe in order to be a Christian? You need to know that you need salvation, help, or deliverance. You must not try to reform yourself or decide that you're going to become a moral person so that God will be impressed. Because he is completely holy, that is, perfectly moral, you have to give up any idea that you can be good enough to meet his standard. This is the *good* bad news. It's bad news because it tells you that you're in an impossible situation that you cannot change. But it's also good news because it will free you from endless cycles of self-improvement that end in ultimate failure.

You also need to trust that what you're unable to do—live a perfectly holy life— he's done for you. This is the *good* good news. This is the gospel. Basically the gospel is the story of how God looked down through the corridors of time and set his love on his people. At a specific point in time, he sent his Son into the world to become fully like us. This is the story you hear about at Christmas. This baby grew to be a man, and after thirty years of obscurity he began to show the people who he was. He did this by performing miracles, healing the sick, and raising the dead. He also demonstrated his deity by teaching people what God required of them and continually foretold his coming death and resurrection. And he did one more thing: he claimed to be God.

Because of his claim to be God, the leading religious people, along with the political powers of the day, passed an unjust sentence of death upon him. Although he had never done anything wrong, he was beaten, mocked, and shamefully executed. He died. Even though it looked like he had failed, the truth is that this was God's plan from the very beginning.

His body was taken down from the cross and laid hastily in a rock tomb in a garden. After three days, some of his followers went to go properly care for his remains and discovered that he had risen from the dead. They actually spoke with him, touched him, and ate with him. This is the story that we celebrate at Easter. After another forty days, he was taken back up into heaven, still in his physical form, and his followers were told that he would return to earth in just the same way.

I told you that there are two things you need to know and believe. The first is that you need more significant help than you or any other merely human person could ever supply. The second is that you believe that Jesus, the Christ, is the person who will supply that help and that if you come to him, he will not turn his back on you. You don't need to understand much more than that, and if you really believe these truths, your life will be transformed by his love.

Below I've written out some verses from the Bible for you. As you read them, you can talk to God, just as though he were sitting right by you (because his presence is everywhere) and ask him for help to understand. Remember, your help isn't based on your ability to perfectly understand or on anything that you can do. If you trust him, he's promised to help you, and that's all you need to know for now.

For all have sinned and fall short of the glory of God. (Rom. 3:23)

For the wages of sin is death, but the free gift of God is eternal life in Christ Jesus our Lord. (Rom. 6:23)

For while we were still weak, at the right time Christ died for the ungodly. For one will scarcely die for a righteous person—though perhaps for a good person one would dare even to die—but God shows his love for us in that while we were still sinners, Christ died for us. (Rom. 5:6–8)

For our sake he made him to be sin who knew no sin, so that in him we might become the righteousness of God. (2 Cor. 5:21)

If you confess with your mouth that Jesus is Lord and believe in your heart that God raised him from the dead, you will be saved. For with the heart one believes and is justified, and with the mouth one confesses and is saved. For the Scripture says, "Everyone who believes in him will not be put to shame." . . . The same Lord is Lord of all, bestowing his riches on all who call on him. For "everyone who calls on the name of the Lord will be saved." (Rom. 10:9–13)

Whoever comes to me I will never cast out. (John 6:37)

Therefore, if anyone is in Christ, he is a new creation. The old has passed away; behold, the new has come. (2 Cor. 5:17)

Come to me, all who labor and are heavy laden, and I will give you rest. Take my yoke upon you, and learn from me, for I am gentle and lowly in heart, and you will find rest for your souls. (Matt. 11:28–29)

There is therefore now no condemnation for those who are in Christ Jesus. (Rom. 8:1)

If you'd like to, you might pray a prayer something like this:

Dear God,

I'll admit that I don't understand everything about this, but I do believe these two things: I need help, and you want to help me. I confess that I'm like Elyse and have pretty much ignored you my whole life, except when I was in trouble or just wanted to feel good about myself. I know that I haven't loved you or my neighbor, so it's true that I deserve to be punished and really do need help. But I also believe that you've brought me here, right now, to read this page, because you are willing to help me and that if I ask you for help, you won't send me away empty-handed. I'm beginning to understand how you punished your Son in my place and how, because of his sacrifice for me, I can have a relationship with you.

Father, please guide me to a good church and help me understand your Word. I give my life to you and ask you to make me yours. In Jesus's name, Amen.

Here are two more thoughts. In his kindness, Jesus established his church to encourage and help us to understand and live out these two truths. If you know that you need help and you think that Jesus is able to supply that help, or if you're still questioning but want to know more, please search out a good church in your neighborhood and begin to make relationships there. A good church is one that recognizes that we cannot save ourselves by our own goodness and that relies wholly on Jesus Christ (and no one else) for this salvation.

You can call around and ask these questions, or you can even go on the Internet and get a listing of churches in your area. Usually a church's website will have something called a "Statement of Faith," from which you can get information about the church. Mormons and Jehovah's Witnesses are not Christian churches, and they do not believe in the gospel (though they might tell you they do), so you don't want to go there. Finding a good church is sometimes quite a process, so don't be discouraged if you don't succeed right away. Keep trying and believing that God will help you.

Second, another factor that will help you grow in this new life of faith is to begin to read what God has said about himself and about us in his Word, the Bible. In the New Testament (the last one-third or so of the Bible), there are four Gospels or narratives about the life of Jesus. I recommend that you start with the first one, Matthew, and then work your way through the other three. I recommend that you purchase a good modern translation, such as the English Standard Version, but you can get any version (though not a paraphrase) that you're comfortable with and begin reading more right away.

The last request that I have of you is that you contact me through my website, www.elysefitzpatrick.com, if you've decided while reading this book that you want to follow Jesus. Thank you for taking time to read this little explanation of the most important news you'll ever hear. You can begin to trust that the Lord will help you understand and become what he wants you to be: a person who's been so loved by him that you're transformed in both your identity and your life.

Notes

Introduction: Are You a Christian Parent?

1. Brent Kunkle cites "the most recent and most cited studies" that he could find about the percentages of youth who leave the church once they're out of the home: 88 percent (The Southern Baptist Convention's Family Life Council study, 2002); 70 percent (LifeWay Research study, 2007; LifeWay also found only 35 percent eventually return); 66 percent (Assemblies of God study); 61 percent (Barna study, "Most Twentysomethings Put Christianity on the Shelf," 2006) in "How Many Youth Are Leaving the Church?" (http://www.conversantlife.com/theology/how-many-youth-are-leaving-the-church).

2. http://www.lifeway.com/lwc/article_main_page/0,1703,A=16594 9&M=200906,00.html.

3. Julius J. Kim, "Rock of Ages: Exodus 17:1–7," in *Heralds of the King: Christ-Centered Sermons in the Tradition of Edmund P. Clowney*, ed. Dennis E. Johnson (Wheaton, IL: Crossway, 2009), 88.

4. Michael S. Horton, *Joel Osteen and the Glory Story: A Case Study*. Part of a collection of essays written by Dr. Horton after his interview on *60 Minutes*, which aired October 14, 2007.

5. Sally Lloyd-Jones, *The Jesus Storybook Bible: Every Story Whispers His Name* (Grand Rapids, MI: ZonderKidz, 2007), 14–17; emphasis added.

Chapter 1: From Sinai to Calvary

1. Gerhard O. Forde, *On Being a Theologian of the Cross: Reflections on Luther's Heidelberg Disputation, 1518* (Grand Rapids, MI: Eerdmans, 1997), 23.

2. We were first introduced to categories such as these in Martin Luther's discourse on Galatians. Although the categories we've chosen are a bit different from his, we gleaned the idea of lower levels of law and obedience from his thought. Martin Luther, *Galatians: Crossway Classic Commentaries*, ed. Alister McGrath (Wheaton, IL: Crossway), 1998.

3. Forde, *On Being a Theologian*, 23.

4. In *Heralds of the King*, Julius Kim describes his training in Christ-centered preaching. One of his professors, Derke Bergsma, taught him: "If a Rabbi can preach your sermon, it isn't a Christian sermon" (Julius J. Kim, "Rock of Ages: Exodus 17:1–7," in *Heralds of the King: Christ-Centered Sermons in the Tradition of Edmond P. Clowney*, ed. Dennis E. Johnson [Wheaton, IL: Crossway, 2009], 90). Although the analogy isn't exact, because parents also need to instruct their children in basic life skills, the primary message of Christian parents needs to differ radically from that of moralistic unbelievers.

5. Tullian Tchividian, *Surprised by Grace: God's Relentless Pursuit of Rebels* (Wheaton, IL: Crossway), 2010.

Chapter 2: How to Raise Good Kids

1. Martin Luther, *Concerning Christian Liberty* (Gloucestershire, UK: Dodo Press, 2008), 12.

2. Sally Lloyd-Jones, *Jesus Storybook Bible: Every Story Whispers His Name* (Grand Rapids, MI: ZonderKidz), 20.

3. Common grace is "God's genuine affection [that] has been poured out upon all persons regardless of who they are or what wrongs they may have done. As Jesus said, God 'causes his sun to rise on the evil and the good, and sends rain on the righteous and the unrighteous' (Matt. 5:45)." James Montgomery Boice, "Common Grace," http://ldolphin.org/common.html.

4. Heidelberg Catechism, question and answer #60.

5. "For truly in this city there were gathered together against your holy servant Jesus, whom you anointed, both Herod and Pontius Pilate, along with the Gentiles and the peoples of Israel, to do whatever your hand and your plan had predestined to take place" (Acts 4:27–28).

6. We're not saying that sin or disobedience is inherently good. We are saying that our inevitable sin is an occasion to turn our eyes upon Jesus once again and be thankful for all he's already done.

Chapter 3: This Is the Work of God

1. Martin Luther, cited in Gerhard O. Forde, *On Being a Theologian of the Cross: Reflections on Luther's Heidelberg Disputation, 1518* (Grand Rapids, MI: Eerdmans, 1997), 127.

2. "Why Are Parents So Quick to Criticize Themselves?" (http://family.custhelp.com/cgi-bin/family.cfg/enduser/prnt_faquid+698&p). Leslie Leyland Fields, *"Parenting Is Your Highest Calling" And 8 Other Myths That Trap Us in Worry and Guilt* (Colorado Springs, CO: Waterbrook, 2008), 5.

Chapter 4: Jesus Loves All His Little Prodigals and Pharisees

1. Gerhard O. Forde, *On Being a Theologian of the Cross: Reflections on Luther's Heidelberg Disputation, 1518* (Grand Rapids, MI: Eerdmans, 1997), 27.

2. *Jesus Loves Me* is a Christian hymn written by Anna B. Warner. The lyrics first appeared as a poem in the context of a novel called *Say and Seal*, written by Susan Warner and published in 1860. The tune was added in 1862 by William Batchelder Bradbury, who found the text of "Jesus Loves Me" in a book, in which the words were spoken as a comforting poem to a dying child. Along with his tune, Bradbury added his own chorus, "Yes, Jesus loves me, Yes, Jesus loves me." After publication the song became one of the most popular Christian hymns in churches around the world (http://en.wikipedia.org/wiki/Jesus_Loves_Me).

3. Edward Mote, "My Hope is Built on Nothing Less," 1834.

Chapter 5: Grace That Trains

1. Bryan Chapell, *Holiness by Grace: Delighting in the Joy That Is Our Strength* (Wheaton, IL: Crossway, 2002), 126.

2. Ibid, 117.

3. Ibid.

4. In the Colossians passage, Paul begins his instruction to families in this way: "And whatever you do, in word or deed, do everything *in the name of the Lord Jesus*, giving thanks to God the Father through him. Wives, submit to your husbands, as is fitting *in the Lord*. . . . Children, obey your parents in everything, for this pleases the *Lord*. Fathers, do not provoke your children, lest they become discouraged" (3:17–18; 20–21). The context for all familial relationships is "in the Lord."

5. Paul ordinarily uses *kurios* (translated "Lord" in our passage) of the Lord Jesus.

6. Titus 1:5–6 reads, "This is why I left you in Crete, so that you might put what remained into order, and appoint elders in every town as I directed you—if anyone is above reproach, the husband of one wife, and his children are believers and not open to the charge of debauchery or insubordination." Although there is much

disagreement about the appropriate interpretation of this passage, the *ESV Study Bible* notes are helpful here: 'His children are believers' can also be rendered 'his children are faithful' (Gk. *pistos*). The primary argument for rendering it as 'believers' is that in the letters to Timothy and Titus, this word almost always refers to 'saving faith.' Those who think it should be rendered "faithful" would argue that no father can guarantee the conversion of his own children, but he can ordinarily ensure that they act in a 'faithful' way. Also, the parallel passage in 1 Timothy 3 says only that the children must be well behaved, not that their conversion is a requirement for their father to be an overseer. The concern in the passage is that the children behave appropriately and are not open to the charge of debauchery or insubordination. The word 'children' (pl. of Gk. *teknon*) would apply only to children living at home and still under their father's authority." (*ESV Study Bible* [Wheaton, IL: Crossway, 2008], 2348).

7. Along these same lines, in Galatians 4:2–3 Paul writes that a father assigns "guardians and managers" to oversee the training of his son.

8. See also 1 Cor. 4:14: "I do not write these things to make you ashamed, but to admonish you as my beloved children"; 1 Thess. 2:11–12: "For you know how, like a father with his children, we exhorted each one of you and encouraged you and charged you to walk in a manner worthy of God, who calls you into his own kingdom and glory."

Chapter 6: Wisdom Greater Than Solomon's

1. Edmund P. Clowney, *Preaching Christ in All of Scripture* (Wheaton, IL: Crossway, 2003), 147.

2. "The Greek text does not specify whether these were two men or a man and a woman (perhaps a husband and a wife) walking together" (*ESV Study Bible*, notes on Luke 24:25 [Wheaten: IL, Crossway, 2008], 2013). Although we don't know who accompanied Cleopas, it would be just like the Savior to visit with his aunt and uncle, particularly since Mary, his aunt, had been there at his crucifixion.

3. Clowney, *Preaching Christ*, 32.

4. Dennis E. Johnson, *Heralds of the King: Christ-Centered Sermons in the Tradition of Edmund P. Clowney* (Wheaton, IL: Crossway, 2009), 28.

5. Sally Lloyd-Jones, *The Jesus Storybook Bible: Every Story Whispers His Name* (Grand Rapids, MI: ZonderKidz, 2007).

6. There are other verses where the rod and physical correction are referenced, but these are aimed at adults who need correction rather than at children.

7. Some parents prefer to use a rod or stick to administer correction. While it is true that Proverbs does use the term "rod"(actually branch or stick) and many people believe that using their hand is inappropriate or unbiblical, we think that

this is a matter of choice. Some make the point that the child will fear the parents' hand if discipline is administered in that way. Whether that is true is not provable, as is the premise that a child will be tempted to sinful fear if a parent disciplines him physically.

8. Of course, there are children who are settled in patterns of rebellion and defiance no matter how much we try to discipline them. You can find help especially geared toward these kinds of recalcitrant children in Elyse Fitzpatrick and Jim Newheiser, *When Good Kids Make Bad Choices* (Eugene, OR: Harvest), 2005.

9. Martin Luther, *Galatians*, Crossway Classic Commentaries, ed. Alister McGrath (Wheaton, IL: Crossway, 1998), 177.

10. Ibid., 148.

11. Bryan Chapell, *Holiness by Grace: Delighting in the Joy That Is Our Strength* (Wheaton, IL: Crossway, 2002), 120.

12. Ibid., 129.

13. See also Rom. 8:12–17.

14. Prov. 1:8, 10, 15; 2:1; 3:1, 21; 4:10, 20; 5:1, 20; 6:1, 3, 20; 7:1; 19:27; 23:15, 19, 26; 24:13, 21; 27:11; 31:2.

15. Both father *and* mother are responsible to teach their children wisdom (Prov. 1:8; 6:20).

Chapter 7: The One Good Story

1. John Calvin, *Institutes of the Christian Religion*, ed. John T. McNeill (Philadelphia, PA: Westminster Press, 1960), 3.7.5.

2. We are a homeschooling family. That doesn't mean that we think that homeschooling is the only option for every Christian home. In some homes it is simply not possible for a myriad of reasons. In other homes, it's a great option, and one that some parents and children excel in. The many options that are available regarding our kids' education is not something we're going to address here, because we think that the gospel allows for each one. We think that some public schools, some Christian or private schools, and some home schools are great. We also think there are dangers and pitfalls in each, and parents have to seek to apply the cross in every choice with every child. However, whether you've decided for homeschool, private or Christian school, or public school, your primary purpose should be to fulfill the beloved Son's commands of loving your neighbor and spreading the good news about him.

3. See also Ex. 34:16; Neh. 13:1–3; and Ezra 9:2: "For they have taken some of their daughters to be wives for themselves and for their sons, so that the holy race has mixed itself with the peoples of the lands."

4. Rahab the harlot and Ruth the Moabitess are perfect examples of gracious redemption and intermarriage between former pagans and Israelites. There are

also examples of the folly of intermarriage between believers and idolaters, such as between Solomon and his pagan wives (1 Kings 11:4).

5. *ESV Study Bible*, notes on 1 Cor. 7:14 (Wheaton, IL: Crossway, 2008), 2200.

6. Paul also commands those who are yet to be married to do so "only in the Lord" (1 Cor. 7:39). I've done enough counseling of women who married unbelievers and suffered significant struggles because of it to know that failure to obey in this area occasions great heartache.

7. "[Unequally yoked with unbelievers] is thus an image for being allied or identified wrongly with unbelievers. In context, it refers especially to those who are still rebelling against Paul *within* the church, whom Paul now shockingly labels as unbelievers." *ESV Study Bible*, notes on 2 Cor. 6:14 (2231; emphasis added).

8. Because every child's spirituality and maturity are different, it's important to know the kinds of temptations that will be most difficult for your child. For instance, if your child is terribly tempted by Andrew's lewd jokes, then, after warning him several times, perhaps you will have to put an end to the relationship. But our goal as the beloved Son's bride is never to cut ourselves off from "sinners"; rather, it is to establish appropriate yet loving relationships with them. We are commanded to go "into" all the world.

9. Probably from Menander's comedy *Thais*, (*PC Study Bible*, note on 1 Cor. 15:33).

10. C. S. Lewis, *The Joyful Christian* (New York: Collier, 1977), 80.

11. Unpublished correspondence from Pastor David Fairchild in 2010. Used by permission.

12. Calvin, *Institutes* 3.7.5.

Chapter 8: Go and Tell Your Father

1. Andrew Murray, *With Christ in the School of Prayer* (London: James Nisbet, 1887), 26.

2. Ibid., 43.

3. Ibid., 25.

4. Paul Miller, *A Praying Life: Connecting with God in a Distracting World* (Colorado Springs, CO: NavPress, 2009), 59.

5. John Calvin, *John, Part 1*, Calvin's Bible Commentaries (Forgotten Books, 2007), 171 (http://www.forgottenbooks.org).

Chapter 9: Weak Parents and Their Strong Savior

1. Dave Harvey, unpublished sermon notes. Used by permission.

2. See also Ps. 115:1; Rom. 16:27; Gal. 1:5; Eph. 3:21; 1 Tim. 1:17; 2 Tim. 4:17–18; Heb. 13:20–21; 2 Pet. 3:17; Jude 25; Rev. 1:5–6; 4:11; 5:11–13; 19:6–7. God used Paul's previous

identity as Saul, the murderous persecutor of the church, to glorify himself: "The saying is trustworthy and deserving of full acceptance, that Christ Jesus came into the world to save sinners, of whom I am the foremost. But I received mercy *for this reason*, that in me, as the foremost, Jesus Christ might *display his perfect patience* as an example to those who were to believe in him for eternal life. To the King of ages, immortal, invisible, the only God, be honor and glory forever and ever. Amen" (1 Tim. 1:15–17). How many times has your heart been encouraged by Peter's denial of the Lord and the Lord's welcome and restoration of him? God uses Peter's great sin to demonstrate what a great Savior he is.

3. F. W. Krummacher, *The Suffering Savior* (Carlisle, PA: Banner of Truth, 2004), 9–10.

4. Although God rules sovereignly over our sin, he is not responsible for it. We are responsible for our sin; he is not. Yet, there is a place where our sin and his sovereignty intersect for his glory. This intersection between our responsibility and his sovereignty is called "concurrence."

5. Much of what we have to say in this section was preached by Dave Harvey and accessed at http://www.metrolife.org/messages.html.

6. Paul Barnett, *The Message of 2 Corinthians* (Downers Grove, IL: InterVarsity, 1988), 178.

Chapter 10: Resting in Grace

1. Martin Luther, *Galatians*, Crossway Classic Commentaries (Wheaton, IL: Crossway, 2003), 33.

2. From the description of Gary Chapman and Ross Campbell, *The Five Love Languages of Children*, at Amazon. This book was listed as the best-selling book on Christian parenting.

3. From an Amazon reviewer of Gary and Anne Marie Ezzo, *Growing Kids God's Way: Biblical Ethics for Parenting* (Louisiana: MO: Growing Families International, 2002). We realize that the Ezzos are not responsible for what Amazon reviewers say about their books, but it's instructive that one consistent result of reading their books is strong parental self-confidence. On their website they say, "*Growing Kids God's Way* can help any parent reach the heart of children with virtues and values that flow from the character of God and do it without stressing the child or the parents."

4. Sinclair Ferguson, *By Grace Alone* (Lake Mary, FL: Reformation Trust, 2010), *xv*.

5. Luther, *Galatians*, 33.

General Index

Scripture Index